MY FATHER'S CLOSET

My Father's Closet

Karen A. McClintock

TRILLIUM, AN IMPRINT OF
THE OHIO STATE UNIVERSITY PRESS
COLUMBUS

Library of Congress Cataloging-in-Publication Data
Names: McClintock, Karen A., 1953– author.
Title: My father's closet / Karen A. McClintock.
Description: Columbus : Trillium, an imprint of The Ohio State University Press, [2017]
Identifiers: LCCN 2016052441 | ISBN 9780814213322 (cloth ; alk. paper) | ISBN 0814213324 (cloth ; alk. paper)
Subjects: LCSH: McClintock, Karen A., 1953—Family. | Psychologists—Biography. | McClintock, Charles Marvin, 1921–1987. | Closeted gays—Family relationships. | Gay fathers—Family relationships. | Gay men—Relations with heterosexual women. | Family secrets. | Bisexuality in marriage.
Classification: LCC BF109.M363 A3 2017 | DDC 977.1/570420922 [B]—dc23
LC record available at https://lccn.loc.gov/2016052441

Cover design by Angela Moody
Text design by Juliet Williams
Type set in Adobe Sabon

9 8 7 6 5 4 3 2 1

*We ought to come away from our storytelling
struck by the sheer chanciness of what happened,
aware that it didn't have to be that way.*

—Joan Chittister and Rowan Williams, *Uncommon Gratitude*

Contents

Acknowledgments

I felt my father's encouraging presence as I spent every Monday for several years searching for the truth. My mother clearly wanted the story to be told when she packed his journals and letters into a box for me to discover. My sister, Marsha, has provided archival and heuristic research, and I have cherished her support. I also thank Duane, who offered open-hearted insights.

My gratitude extends to my editor and friend Beth Gaede, who has also assisted me with previous books; to Jennifer Margulis, a very wise consultant; to copy editor Marcia Hunter; and to Candace Walsh, who taught me to tell my own story in the book while working her magic as developmental editor.

As the book and our family story finds completion, I thank Megan for her abundant love and faith in me. My husband, Mick, was a gem throughout the project—listening to sections as they emerged and giving me freedom to create a work that healed me. He shows up fully without secrets or pretenses, and to this day wears my father's gold wedding band. I also want to thank many personal friends and colleagues for supporting the project.

The book has been edited to include both actual and fictional names, safeguarding those who may have compelling needs for privacy. Lastly, I want to thank the University Press, enthusiastic editor Tony Sanfilippo, and his publication team, who welcomed the book, my father, and me back home to Columbus and to the university.

Prologue

Miss Wyeth, our sixth-grade Sunday school teacher, expected every child in her class to pick a favorite Bible verse. Most kids picked familiar sentences like "God so loved the world" or "Nothing can separate us from the love of God," but my favorite verse to this day is actually Jesus' question to Pilate: "And what is truth?" This choice puzzled my librarian mother who strongly believed in historical fiction. Her well-crafted version of our family story helped us to survive in an untenable situation—during a time in history when the truth would have been impossible to navigate.

All the things I want to tell you in this memoir are true—the storybook marriage and the disintegration of my parents' intimacy, my idyllic childhood, and the damage of knowing very little about my father. As a child I liked him with undiscerning fondness. The secretive dad showed up one day while I was sitting at my desk.

The previous evening I had been sitting with four other women in my writing group in the living room of my crumbling Victorian rental home when our writing teacher, Susan, asked us to consider our "muse." "Who is it?" she asked, "Living or dead, who wants you to write—who wants you to tell your story or their story?" Veronica knew right away; both Rebecca and Rhoda were certain too; Natalie and I said we'd have to get back to her on this. The next morning, with my mint tea in an oversized mug and my soft terry-cloth robe wrapped around me, I went to my desk on the rickety sunporch on the second floor. The room slanted slightly toward the alley, as if one day it would separate itself from the house altogether. Meanwhile, I occupied it with an old desk I'd refinished and stacked it with books safely tucked away from water that leaked down the outside walls during the rainy months. I sat down on my swivel chair and listened to Susan's voice: "Who wants you to tell their story?" Dad appeared in the doorway, ducking down slightly to fit his six-foot-two frame beneath the six-foot clearance. I won't pontificate about whether I believe in ghosts, or the Holy Spirit, or reappearances by the dead. I can't prove anything; I learned that growing up in a family where the truth was slippery.

I just know he was there. It was 1994. I had crash-landed in this old Victorian house after a painful divorce, drug dealers next door cooked meth at night, and it took a crew of five friends to scrape eight wallpaper layers off the plaster walls in the bedroom my twelve-year-old needed to decorate her way. She had nightmares in that house, where the heavy leaded windows creaked and only partially shut. Perhaps we were both aware that spirits and the house seemed to go hand in hand. It was quaintly beautiful, with wood floors that slanted slightly eastward, and the stairs to our rooms were so off-kilter that I often leaned against the wall on the way up. We had a crazy and lovable little fox terrier we called Maggie, the name I'd wanted for my daughter but lost the toss on. While the black-and-white dog's swirling energy helped to ease our grief at the family breakup, the house seemed more haunted than quaint.

Standing in the doorway, Dad didn't say anything that day. And I wasn't afraid of him. Rather, I was heartsick for the bodily form I would have rushed to and grabbed around the waist and clung to. "Okay, Dad," I said, rather formally, as was our custom in life. "It's good to have you show up like this." He's the last person I expected to become my muse, knowing how much energy it took him to keep his own life entirely to himself. Maggie came running out onto the little porch, and I'd swear Dad leaned over to pet her. And then he disappeared.

WINGED CUPID

ALICE LIVINGSTON   CHARLES MARVIN McCLINTOCK

Chapter 1

Winged Cupid

1967

At age fourteen, I am bothered by zits and mood swings. Searching through every bookshelf in the house for information about sex, I find an utterly useless and too-heavy-to-lift textbook by Alfred Kinsey and a collection of *National Geographic* magazines containing pictures but no instructions. So I ask Mom about falling in love, which seems like an acceptable topic that might lead her to tell me more about sex.

"I'm sure I must have told you this before," she says flatly, reaching under the end table to the bottom shelf for visual aids—pulling out her 1938 North High School yearbook. Folded clippings from *The Columbus Journal* are stuck between the pages. Mom pats the spot next to her on the lime green couch that backs up to the picture window. A thin film of sheer draperies keeps curious neighbors from knowing too much about us. She offers her palm-out finger wiggle, the come-here gesture that I cherished as a child and have resisted since becoming a teenager. I'm reluctant to move closer to the lingering smell of smoke in her hair and on her clothing, even though she put the last butt out a few minutes ago. The pictures are the hook that draws me over to her.

Looking at her senior picture a long while, I unsuccessfully try to find my face inside hers. Her head is tilted leftward, and she looks over her shoulder at the camera, giving off a bit of sass. She has approachably friendly features that neither stand out nor offend.

"You're so young, Mom," I say.

She flips the book forward to my father's senior picture, and I think that his baby-fine hair is like mine. I reach up and rake my fingers through my bangs the way men do in the movies when they try to catch a look from a group of girls walking by. I've never seen Dad do that, so I squint at his picture in case I missed something.

"Not a hair out of place," Mom says. "Not then, not ever." She has a slightly disapproving tone to her voice.

"His glasses make him look smart," I say, though he also looks slightly nerdy and naïve.

"He's sweet looking, isn't he?" she asks. "The smile is what got me."

I stop my usual chatty banter, knowing that the less I say the more she will. She's about to launch into the story of their romance. Telling it reminds her that while the smile reeled her in, she married him for love, for his inviting blue eyes, the resonant tone in his voice, and his fascination with her.

Thinking back on this day, the adult me wants to derail her story, to interrupt it by swapping my father for one of those other boys in the yearbook, to pick out Ben for her or Ralph, Roger, maybe Mike. I'd find a totally different guy to meet her at the top of the stairs at the high school the day she won the election and became membership recruiter for the Thespian Society, the job that led her directly into my father's charms. If I could reach back in time and disrupt their story, I could save them those years of heartache.

But I can't. Besides, I wouldn't exist if it had gone differently.

So I'm content with the memory of sitting next to her looking at the yearbook, exploring young love's innocence and trickery.

I am nearly all grown up. I play with my Barbie doll in secret since I am too mature for such things. I've still got her, though. I've hidden her away in the back of my closet along with Ken, her supposed boyfriend, who has some bald spots in his felt hair. I don't know what she sees in him. My Barbie can be reckless when she's in love.

"Here's how I remember it," Mom says.

I am under orders to call her *Mom* when we are at home, *Mother* in the presence of elderly parents or the minister from the church, and *Mommy*—never, ever *Mommy*. She says kids who use *Mommy* are whining. She doesn't like the nasal twang of *Momma* either, because it takes her back to the shabby farmhouse where she was raised on the Kentucky-Ohio border, a past she prefers to forget.

I tuck my feet up on the couch, and she tilts to the left so I can slip them beneath her.

"I was so happy to be back in school after a summer of house-cleaning and cooking for the boarding students at our house that I took the stairs two at a time to the top floor at school and raced into the drama classroom," she says.

"The first thing you notice in that room is a portrait of Shakespeare, who is sometimes called 'the old Bard,'" she says, always making use of a teachable moment. "I stared at that picture during boring classes. He had a very long nose and a receding hairline, and you couldn't see his neck under his large, white collar. I swear he winked at me sometimes."

She winks at me twice to demonstrate, and the winking widens her smile.

"There was a quote by him on the wall above the chalkboard from *A Midsummer Night's Dream,* which, by the way, you'll have to read in high school. It read, 'Love looks not with the eyes, but with the mind, and therefore is winged Cupid painted blind.' And that, my dear, is the truth about love."

Truth is terribly complicated in our household. So I flip through the pages of the yearbook.

"What's this smoke stack thing, Mom?" I ask.

She laughs. "Before the building became North High School, it was a sewer pipe factory."

She reaches over for a cigarette, taps one toward the end of the box, looks over at me, shrugs, and sets it aside. I take a deeper breath.

"The drama room had high vaulted ceilings and hardwood floors that were all splattered with paint from set building."

I know about backdrops and painted flats. Mom and Dad have taken my older sister, Marsha, and me to plays since we were old enough to sit still for a few hours. We had annual family subscriptions to the college theater, and when Broadway tours came to town, my father was first in line for tickets. I also had starring roles in a community theater the previous two summers, playing a large costumed beagle at age twelve and a dancing harlot in a play about Gideon at age thirteen. We stuffed socks into the spangled bras of our belly-dancing outfits. I love hearing Mom talk about the theater; it's in our DNA.

Mom takes the book back onto her lap and finds a picture of a North High School production of *Macbeth*. "There we are," she says. "Now back to our first meeting of the Thespian Society."

"Are you supposed to say that word, Mom?"

"Yes honey, it's not . . ." She paused to avoid that other word. "At your school it's called Drama Club. A thespian is an actor, someone who plays a role in a play. Okay, where was I?"

"You're at the meeting."

"All my friends were saying 'hi' and asking, 'How was your summer?' and such. I hung my coat on a clothes rack next to shirts with grimy orange makeup on them and dropped my books on a pile of old shoes."

"Was Dad there?"

"No, honey, be patient. He comes along later."

I figure she wants another cigarette, since I annoy her with too many questions, but she doesn't budge.

"The room had those flip-down chairs you sometimes see in movie theaters. I liked to push them down and let them snap back as I walked down the aisle to find my seat."

I raise one eyebrow at her, a skill she taught me. It makes us look skeptical and wise at the same time.

"I wasn't afraid to be the center of attention. I took a seat in the middle section. I felt butterflies that day, like something good was going to happen—like the moment when the curtain is about to rise."

"Our meeting was called to order by a student teacher named Robbie who still had freckles and wore All-Star sneakers. He sat on the edge of the teacher's desk and read from a clipboard."

"Okay, well, let's elect our officers," she says, playing Robbie, then switching back to her own voice. Mom could have been a voice-over actor. Even in ordinary conversations she changes her tone and cadence to fit the character. Robbie sounds like a bratty kid.

"I stopped paying attention and looked around the room for my friends. Let me show you some of them." She flips forward to pages with girls' pictures.

"Meet Helen," she says, poking at the page a little emphatically.

"Helen got all the best roles because she was so beautiful, innocent, and sexy."

"Not as sexy as you, Mom," I say.

"Sexy isn't all it's cracked up to be, dear," she says, and sighs like she does when she takes a long drag.

"Here's Martha. She played the strange and scary parts, old hags who live nearby . . . maybe right here in our neighborhood." Her voice is resonant and spooky.

"Martha played the wife of Drrrracula," she says, rolling the *r* in my direction.

I lean into her and cuddle up for protection just for a minute.

"I can see why," I say. "She looks like a kid down the street whose nose has been broken a few times."

"She was a good actress; we have to give her that." Mom has a knack for saying something nice about everyone.

"Were you in a play?" I ask.

"Not interested in the limelight."

I look over at her. She has the class and beauty of a movie actress, with ample hips and thighs, full and rounded breasts. Her auburn hair falls in wide curls to her shoulders.

"I've always thought of myself as ordinary," she says. "I prefer to play supportive roles. I take the behind-the-scenes jobs like stage manager. During a revival of *No, No, Nanette,* I calmed an actor with stage fright and coached the director on ways to handle the neurotic lead."

"But anyway," she says, realizing we've strayed from the story again, "we elected officers for the year, and then Robbie waved his clipboard to get us to settle down. He announced one more role he had to fill. 'We need a membership recruiter,' he said. I knew right away that I wanted the job. I'd already been recruiting stagehands, house managers, and ushers. 'I'm voting for Alice,' my friend Tom shouted from the back of the room. 'She could sell New Yorkers the Brooklyn Bridge.' And everyone laughed, saying, 'That's right,' and 'Uh, huh.'"

"Good thing you can take a joke."

"The job turned out to be fun and easy, except for your dad. I had to hound him like crazy before I got him to sign up. He wanted me to keep pestering him."

I know Mom can be pretty persuasive; for two years in a row she's gotten gold ribbons as the regional winner in overall cookie sales among Girl Scout troop leaders.

"At the end of the meeting, Robbie announced auditions for the fall play. It was my job to distribute scripts to interested actors. I scooped them up and headed for the door with my friend Peg, who was sure to audition for the ingénue. Like most high school theaters, we didn't have enough boys for the male roles. As we walked home that day I told her, 'I have my eye on a boy named Charles in my English class, who can read Shakespeare as if he understands it. The tone of his voice enchants me.'"

I know exactly what she means about his voice. When I sit on his lap and he reads to me, his whole chest vibrates gently, and I am soothed and lulled into trust. Maybe this is what the love thing feels like.

Mom says that the next day she intentionally blocked the exit at her Classic Literature class, as she points to her friend Peg's picture.

"I flattened myself against the door jamb, which forced your father to pass by me in close range. He seemed disoriented. Maybe it was my perfume."

She's blushing.

"I had to look up at him, of course, and we locked eyes and everything stopped, like you see in the movies. When he squeezed by me, I said, 'Charles, can I talk to you for a minute? I don't want you to be late for class. He said he'd never been late to class before, so maybe he should try it. I went on and on about how well he could read Shakespeare and asked him to sign up for auditions. I remember it like we were in slow motion."

She's off in some dreamy place of deep sighs and half-closed eyelids.

"Everyone around us disappeared. Maybe the bell rang, but I don't remember hearing it. I just kept looking at him until he glanced down the hall and noticed that we were all alone now. 'I'd better go,' he said. As we turned opposite ways, our arms brushed up against each other and I felt a jolt of electricity."

"Yikes," I say. "Were you in trouble for being late to class?"

"Not that I remember. But whatever my teacher had to say that day was lost on me. My brain was back in the hallway with Charles."

"It's funny to hear you call him that."

"Oh, I guess it would be strange. Everyone called him Charles in high school, though he signed letters using his middle name, Marvin. You must have been ten or eleven when he became Mac—a nickname they gave him at work."

A yellowed newspaper clipping falls from the yearbook as she turns another page. I gently unfold it, and zoom in on a man in a villainous black mustache. The caption beneath it reads, "Charles M. McClintock as Col. Bruce in a musical melodrama, *Nick of the Woods*."

"Is this the play you signed him up for?"

"No, that one came later."

I see the fuzzy blue slippers I thought I'd lost hiding under Dad's chair across the living room, so I get up, slip them on, and come flip-flopping back to the couch. Mom also rearranges herself by tucking her feet under her hip on my side, exposing the tops of her knee-high nylons under the stretch pants of her tan pants suit. She puts a pillow against her thigh so that I can lie back on the couch and lean my head against it. I'm more relaxed with her and glad to be closer now that the cigarette smells have faded into the background.

Mom's a librarian, which explains the piles of books at her end of the couch and her familiarity with fiction. She's been working at the reference desk at Grandview Heights Public Library every weekday since I went off to the first grade. On Fridays my sister and I rush home, because that's the day she brings us new books. She appreciates a good story's enchanting effect and crafted some doozies.

"The next day he intentionally found a seat by me. Our English teacher, Mrs. Bryant, began her lecture with a question. 'What words, my dear friends, would Shakespeare have chosen for his gravestone?' After a brief pause, she answered her own question to prime the pump: 'All the world's a stage and we are merely players?' She called on a short guy in the front row. 'To be or not to be?' he asked. 'Possibly,' she said. 'Anyone else?' Mrs. Bryant called on the class clown, who came through with 'Out, out damned spot.' I raised my hand and added, 'To sleep, perchance to dream?' Then your dad looked over at me and chimed in, 'Parting is such sweet sorrow!' He impishly grinned at me—and I felt happily all alone with him in the room.

"Mrs. Bryant let the discussion trail off. 'Students, let's open our text books to *A Midsummer Night's Dream*. We're reading act 4, scene 1, and you remember that the fairies have turned our hero into Bottom the donkey.' She assigned the roles, with your father as the donkey and me as Titania, the love-struck heroine. A narrator was recruited to start reading at the section of the play where Titania gathers nettles and ivy to feed Bottom. I was nervous, of course, but I read Titania's lines like a pro. I memorized those lines years later. Sometimes I said them to you while you fell asleep in your crib."

"Maybe I'll remember them, too," I say, wanting to be like her in every way, wanting to fall in love like she did.

> Sleep thou, and I will wind thee in my arms.
> Fairies, be gone, and be all ways away.
> So doth the woodbine the sweet honeysuckle
> Gently entwist; the female ivy so
> Enrings the barky fingers of the elm.
> O! how I love thee; how I dote on thee!

"I like that, Mom. I didn't know Shakespeare wrote fairy tales."

"All love is a fairy tale, sweetie," she says. "Shush now. Your dad is about to read the next line. He said, 'Now, my Titania; wake you, my sweet queen.' I'm sure I blushed as Mrs. Bryant called a halt to our reading. Then she asked us to stand up for applause. Your father swept an imaginary plumed hat to the side, made a few donkey snorting heehaws, bowed all the way to the floor, and looked at me on his way back up. I made a slight curtsy."

"After the bell rang, he waited for me in the hallway. 'When are the auditions?' he asked. 'Next Tuesday. You'll need a five-minute monologue, maybe one of Bottom's speeches, if you don't mind making an ass out of yourself again.'"

"Mom, you didn't say that. You're making that up. You don't say *ass*."

"How do you know, sweetie? Back then I was a wild one." She's rumpling my hair and tickling my sides.

"Did he audition?"

"Yes, and I told him I'd be there to cheer him on."

1987

Mother takes a long drag on her Pall Mall. She's up to three packs a day at age sixty-four and keeps on smoking despite her diagnosis of lung cancer. She wears a coarse auburn wig in a pixy bob that she purchased from her hairdresser, who, she says proudly, shaped it to her specifications. She is pale and so thin I can see her cheekbones. Her smile wrinkles have disappeared.

We are once again sitting on the lime green couch. By now I have learned about secondhand smoke and the toxicity of secrets, so I sit on the far end and try to breathe without taking in any carcinogens. I've given up asking her not to smoke, and she's given up holding back on my account.

We sit together, looking at more clippings she has found from *The Columbus Dispatch* and *The Ohio Lantern*. Mother carefully unfolds the fragile, yellowed pages with pictures and reviews of my father's various roles in the theater.

"I'm still amazed that he was my leading man for over forty years." She sighs and grabs a tissue.

For six months now she has been living alone, and the memory of his interest in her has become bittersweet. I wait for her to bring up topics she's avoided for years. Father's early interest in my mother contained several detours. The first one was his flirtation with the flouncy Eleanora, whom Mom likes talking about because it proves that she wasn't the only foolish girl to fall for him. She does not like to talk about his other detours, especially a man named Walther.

So instead she reverts to the fairy-tale start of their relationship. She describes sitting in the audience every night during the run of his play, watching him perform the role of the curmudgeon grandfather in *You Can't Take It with You*. On the North High stage, my father let his alter ego help him past his shyness. He played a flamboyant comic in a melodrama, an actor in drag, and a villain hiding behind a curled mustache. For many of those shows, she assisted as the stage manager or handled props while peering around the curtain at the actors on stage. "I spent my life watching him from the wings," she says. She rubs the butt of her cigarette in the ashtray until it goes out and the smoke drifts off. I wonder if she ever wanted more.

Chapter 2

Grandma Wanted a Girl

In 1923 when my father Charles Marvin McClintock was born, his father had successfully risen from poverty to prominence. Daily, except Sundays, my paternal grandfather Chester W. "Chet" McClintock proudly turned the key and unlocked the glass front door to enter his very own pharmacy, the Varsity Drug Store, bordering the campus at Ohio State University. In the back of the shop, wearing his white apron and a pair of magnifying glasses, he mixed together powders that could cure gout, a head cold, or arthritis. Back then, pharmacies were often a first stop for people with illnesses rather than the place the doctor sent them. He became a keen observer of symptoms and likely remedies and studied voraciously to keep current with new elixirs to alleviate anxiety, toothache, or bunion pain.

Grandfather neither questioned God about diseases or life's tragedies, nor expressed emotions that would have gotten in the way of business. Feeling anything could have led him to the lonely heartache connected with his parents' sudden and terrifying deaths. Standing over their freshly dug graves at fifteen, he promised not only to survive, but to secure a bright future for his younger brothers and sister, which to his credit, he did. He was still a young man when he married Clara Bell (who with total disgust and a clipped German accent often said, "My name sounds like the name of a cow! Only a cow should haf this name."), and I presume that he loved her, although none of us ever saw affection between them. Theirs was a loyal and convenient relationship, which my parents' marriage also became.

The story of their meeting and hasty marriage has faded from family memory, and no one took pictures on their wedding day. Their first son, Donald, was a proud duplicate of his father. He was doted on, by all accounts—given the best toys, read to on his mother's lap, taken to school so that he didn't have to ride the bus. She adored him, showed him off to friends, and during the nine years it took for her to become pregnant again, she longed for a girl. She had been raised in a family with girls, who sat for a portrait wearing white dresses with huge blue bows in their hair.

When Charles Marvin came along, tears streamed down Clara's cheeks as she rocked her new baby to sleep. Clara apologized to Chet, "He was supposed to be a girl." Ruminating on the childhood she enjoyed with four sisters, she pined for the dress-up world of ribbons and lace, all of them chatting happily over fine needlework, and their successes and disasters while learning to cook. Loneliness engulfed her. Her first boy was growing up to be a stubborn handful, and, while she loved him dearly, she didn't want to raise another boy.

She called her new boy Marvin, while his father called him Charles-Marvin, as if it were all one word. By the time he was ten, she had taught him to quilt, and she carefully laid out projects for him. "We'll draw and cut out some animals, and you can stitch them onto the fabric. . . . How about that Marvin?"

"Sure, Mom," he said. "I want a giraffe and a tiger," he continued, eager to please her. She drew them in pencil to guide his way. The cotton quilt top and the batting were both white, and his nearly invisible stitches were fine and exact. Since she was most often stern and disciplined, Clara used quilting as a way to draw her son close to the softer parts of her heart. Marvin completed his first full-size bed quilt at age fourteen. It has become yellow with age, but I am pleased to have it still.

Marvin found dirt distasteful, unless it was necessary to join his mother planting flowers in pots she'd brought home from her garden club. He didn't wrestle in the backyard with other boys and used his bike for necessary trips around the neighborhood rather than adventures into unknown territory. He tried his hand at delivering newspapers but detested having to ask for money, so, with her persuasion, "Pop" let him give it up. With his father always at the pharmacy or off at conferences, Marvin didn't throw a ball around the yard or take up fishing. He was raised to companion his mother, who taught him to be a polite and proper boy. During his younger years at school, he was the kid no one noticed.

The Drama Society at North High School opened up his world. Starring as the mustached colonel from Kentucky in *Nick of the Woods,* he was unconstrained. In an assigned role, he could be emotionally flamboyant and funny. When the curtain went up and the floodlights washed over him, he freely explored hilarity, rage, jealousy, or devastating heartache. What might it be like to fling headlong into love and explore the depths of one's passion? Meeting Eleanora and then Alice, he felt relief that there were at least two women in the world who, unlike his emotionally detached mother, felt and expressed their feelings, laughed easily, and said just what they thought.

His senior year in high school, Marvin barely lived at home—going out to movies or live theater every evening where he could escape his parents' emotional austerity. These were also the years he picked up a journal and a pen and became clearer about his relationship with his mother. In the middle of his senior year, he wrote:

I overheard something tonight that explains a lot of things. There was a party going on downstairs. Two of the women were upstairs having a conversation, and I heard Emily Miller say, 'Clara wanted a girl so badly,' and as my mother came into the room, 'Didn't you Clara?' Mother said, 'Yes.' Now I know why she tried to bring me up as a girl in so many ways, why I've been called a sissy so many terrible times, and why she doesn't like me as much as Don. Perhaps it's because he was the first born. I don't blame her, though, for after all it must have been a big disappointment to her. I still love her with all my heart, and I'm sure she loves me too.

2010

Years later, while reading this journal entry, my forehead clenches and I have a hard time making it relax. My father clearly chose to love his mother to the detriment of his self-worth. Overhearing thinly veiled comments about his "difference," he buried his soul before he even reached puberty. I'm left wondering what Clara's friends had said *before* he overheard them. Had they been saying things like, "That Marvin, he's just not like the other boys," or "They should have taken him to a doctor." Did they pity his mother for being stuck with a girlish boy, or blame her for creating one?

As I consider my father's early years, I intuitively fill in the gaps.

If Clara or Chet could have shaped his identity, they would have raised him to be more like Donald—a tough and strongly independent son who joined a conservative patriarchal religion that would normalize his male dominance. Donald and his friends got strong pats on the back from peers and parents alike, but these same adults kept Charles-Marvin at a distance, watched him curiously, and scratched their heads while talking about him behind closed doors.

"Go outside and play now," Clara might have told him on a sunny day, but she wouldn't have convinced him; he'd have stayed behind to see what his mother was up to. And, lonely for company, I think she would also have been glad that he did. Charles-Marvin would have chatted easily with his mother as she set up her easel. When her paints were out on the table, after a bit of begging, he was allowed to mix colors for her, and she gave him paper and brushes.

On the wall behind my dining room table hangs Grandma Clara's full-size watercolor painting of two children sitting at a simple wooden table. The painting shows one boy and one girl bowing their heads, and folding their hands for prayer with food set out before them. Looking at it, I hear Grandpa Chet saying his usual grace, "Lord, for what we are about to receive, make us truly thankful."

Grandma Clara painted it using Donald's picture as her model for the little rascally boy who happens to be looking at the bread rather than closing his eyes. Could Charles-Marvin have wondered as I do now, why it is that when she replicated their family dining table, she'd made the second child a little girl?

Chapter 3

Courtship by Pie

On Mother's side of the family, courtship begins with pie. Grandma Bata (pronounced with two long "a" sounds) caught Grandpa Sam with a luscious double-crust peach pie. And once Alice had "come of age," as they say, Bata perfected her recipes every season, hoping to catch a good husband for her daughter. Inclined to follow her lead, at age forty and newly single, I stocked up on pastry flour and Crisco when one of my girlfriends gave my phone number to a particularly charming man in the neighborhood known as the "divorce recovery guy."

On the morning of our date, I bought juicy strawberries at Safeway and brought them home. The red berries were piled high on my homemade crust and spilled over onto the table until I glued them into place with a delicious warm sauce. When the pie had "set up," I chilled it in the refrigerator for a few hours, while I showered and put on seductive underwear. No male in his right mind could have resisted that pie.

I can hear Grandmother Bata calling out to me from her grave at Union Cemetery in Columbus, where she rests in peace next to my three other grandparents. "You know I love you, sweetie, but you broke two family rules that night: first, the sex part, which you don't seem to be overtly mentioning, and second, using pie like that in an entirely unethical way!"

"Okay, Grandma," I tell her, "things are different these days."

"In a proper relationship, you don't offer the pie on the first date," she says.

Maybe you don't offer sex either, I think in retrospect. Over a month of dating passed before I offered the man I am now married to a double-crust apple pie. It wasn't the only reason he married me, but it helped—Grandma taught me to make a persuasive pie.

Grandma Bata's green *Joy of Cooking* cookbook is still front and center on the shelf in my kitchen. The pages in the pie section have pulled loose from the binding—escaping the mundane sections on appetizers and meat dishes. Several people have offered to buy me new cookbooks when they see the old frayed one, but it holds too many mealtime memories to part with. Family dinners at Grandmother's house teemed with laughter, and Grandma was a keen listener. Whether it was a bowl of beef stew or the pie that followed, they were served with sound advice.

Grandma's pies also kept the family from starving.

When the Great Depression hit Columbus, Ohio, my mother's father, Sam, lost his job as a flooring carpenter. He wasn't just a run-of-the-mill carpenter; Mother boasted that he had laid the flooring in the Rose Room of the White House. I have almost no recollection of him standing up, let alone working. He was either in his chair, leaning toward the arched wooden radio writing down baseball statistics, or sitting at the dining table eating a meal. As kids, we got to sit on his lap when his team was losing, and we'd poke at his round face, rub our hands over his bald head, and try to touch our tongues to our noses the way he could.

During the Depression, their family home expanded at the seams with men living two to a room on the second floor along with Mother's older brother Bill. Mother and her parents were bumped up to the third floor. Grandma Bata arose early to wash linens, clean bathrooms, prepare meals for nine people living in the house, and bake pies, cakes, breads and muffins. Around ten each morning, except Sunday, Grandpa Sam took her pies and pastries in boxes and baskets down the block to High Street and sold them to passersby on the sidewalk at a place he affectionately called the "Livingston Corner Bakery."

They called their three-story brownstone "the boarding house." It sat on the road's curve where Ohio State University fraternity houses bumped into Indianola Presbyterian Church, a formidable grey stone edifice with plenty of stained glass. The building looked more Episcopalian than Presbyterian, but since Grandma picked her churches more by proximity than theology, it suited them just fine for worship and family weddings. Mom told elaborate stories about her high school years in that old neighborhood.

The brownstone had a front porch swing, and every day someone was out there watching the goings on at the fraternities. On Saturday nights, Uncle Bill and some of his roommates cast lots for the swing so they could hold hands and kiss their girlfriends. When chores were finished, the porch became their window on the world, in a neighborhood of carefree students falling in love and testing their limits with alcohol.

"Something interestin' was always going on," Grandma Bata said in her slightly southern drawl.

Grandmother's stories about my parents' courtship are playful and happy. "When your father and mother started dating," she said, "Bill teased Alice relentlessly and plopped himself down on the couch right between them whenever they found private time."

In Dad's journal he wrote, "*Maybe, after the dance tonight I can sit next to Alice on the swing.*" And they might have done just that, unless Bill was around.

"Your father didn't know how to court your mother, since it hadn't gone so well with his first girlfriend, Eleanora," Grandma said.

I have a hard time thinking about my parents as insecure and naïve. I never longed for connection as a teenager, since intimacy had a peculiar twist in my home. My first dates fell on the fear side of adrenalin instead of the excitement side.

"They started dating in earnest the fall of Alice's senior year, and she stopped talking to me for a while," Grandma said. "After school your mother often ran up to the third floor and came back down to join me for pie in the kitchen. As I washed my hands to begin cooking and dried them on my apron, your mother ignored me—sulking and hoping that I wouldn't ask her any nosy questions."

Grandma smiled so constantly that, in her later years, the wrinkles on her face arched upward around her mouth. People saw warmth and generosity all over her. We could count on Grandma. I think of her the way I recall a labor nurse who walked the halls with me at the hospital when I was more than a day into birthing my daughter and exhausted. During a huge contraction, she faced me, wrapped her arms tightly around my back up over the bulging belly and kept me from falling to the floor. My face was smashed against a large, soft pair of breasts, and I could hear her muffled commands. "Breathe, now," she said. "You know what to do, just keep breathing." She was so strong, I gave her all my weight, and I knew it would be all right. That's how Grandma Bata was too. You could lean on her.

(Grandma, from her place in heaven, has given me permission to fill out the story since I've heard it from several viewpoints over the years. She deserves full credit for my skill at this.)

At nineteen, Alice was at that falling-in-love stage when teens don't talk to their parents.

"How was school?" Bata asked.

"Okay." Alice said nothing more.

Bata drew a figure eight in the air with her rolling pin.

"Are you here to help?"

Alice just shrugged, took it, and rolled out a piecrust.

"Heard anything from Johnny lately?"

"Mom, Johnny never even apologized for ruining your pie!"

Alice was happy that Johnny was long gone, but Bata was apparently still interested in him, despite his having ruined a beautiful blackberry pie by forking through it as if it were his personal dinner plate, and leaving it half-eaten on the dining table.

"Obviously, his mother never taught him any manners."

"Mom, he wouldn't have apologized anyway; that's just Johnny. He came over here, plopped his shoes on the furniture in the parlor, and acted like he owned the place. I can't believe you think he's good enough for me!"

"You're right; I think you have better options." She put two finished pies in the oven.

"It's a good thing Johnny got into the University of Pennsylvania, and I didn't even have to break up with him. He stuffed everything he owned into his car, kissed Columbus and me goodbye, put the key into the starter, and drove off."

"But he's writing you letters—missing his girl back home."

Pushing down the cowlick on her forehead, Alice recalled Johnny's taunting words that she wasn't pretty enough to catch an intelligent man.

"I got a letter last week, but I barely read it. I hope I never see Johnny again!" Her tone was getting angrier.

"Okay, then." Bata turned to the sink to start in on pots and pans. "Who would you rather talk about?"

Alice didn't answer the question. She grabbed up her books and took the stairs two at a time. She was interested in Charles Marvin McClintock, but she wasn't ready to talk to her mother about him.

According to his journal, Charles offered to meet Alice at the bus and walk her home, and when they got there, they sat on the ledge of the half-wall that spanned the front porch and chatted for nearly an hour. He laughed at her stories about pranks at the fraternity houses; boys with BB guns shooting out streetlights at night just for the fun of it, and nightly panty raids from one house to the next house so that, when dawn arose, bras and panties were flying atop flagpoles. The boys from Delta Chi sang boisterous drinking songs on their front lawns, and the boys over at Delta Sigma Phi put their beds out on their front porch to "sleep" there on warm starry nights.

Charles joked that she should go over and say "hello" to them.

"I'm on strict limits here, with my brother and his friends in the house watching my every move, so I can't possibly sneak out."

Charles was ready to strike out on his own.

"I'd like to be in a fraternity; it sounds like fun. I've applied for admission to the university, and I would give anything to move into a frat house."

Even when his parents were home, he was lonely there. Donald had joined the military and moved out, his father was always at work, and his mother was a full-time volunteer with every auxiliary she could find.

"How 'bout I move over here into the boarding house when the next boy graduates?" he asked Alice.

"Absolutely not! I can't date boys who live in the house. That wouldn't do at all." Smiling, she leaned toward him until their shoulders and upper arms met.

During a lull in their conversation, Bata poked her head out the screen door and simply asked, "Pie?"

It was both an offer and a manners exam.

"Thanks, Mrs. Livingston. What kind of pie did you bake?"

But she didn't have to answer him. Scents of peach and cinnamon wafted their way through the door and answered his question as Alice and Charles stepped across the threshold and went into the parlor. Charles ate a gentleman's-sized slice and told Bata thank you a half dozen times before heading home.

After their pie date, Charles spent a full year avoiding Alice in classes, at school, and in the theater—still making a go of it with Eleanora. But he was uncertain to the core. He and Eleanora simply lacked romantic spark. Her aloofness was more familiar to him and less threatening than Alice's open-hearted integrity, but he wasn't crazy about her.

I have to keep telling myself that he was just nineteen. No one knows much about love at nineteen. And he hadn't had a good start at attachment. He was lonely and going more for "the look" of a good relationship than genuine connection—a skill he developed young and perfected throughout his life. I painfully repeated the pattern.

But eventually, he yearned for more than what he had with a brainless prima donna. He picked up the phone, and called Alice.

"I'll get it!" Alice yelled, racing the extra flights down to the parlor. Her friend Brenda had told her Charles might be calling. She extended her elbows out in self-defense as she passed the second floor. "Get out of the way!" she yelled as her brother Bill came down the hall.

"What's gotten into you?" he asked as she flew by.

She lifted the handle, took a deep breath, and said, "Hello?"

"Hello, it's Charles."

"Where've you been? I thought maybe you fell in." She didn't want to sound as eager as she felt.

"I've sorted out a few things." He said this without a hint of defensiveness. He doesn't wander around in words. "Would you like to go to homecoming with me?"

"Yes."

Charles went to the University Flower Shop on the day of the dance. He was very picky about flowers and colors, so he never let the owner, Sid, help him with his choice. He'd memorized Alice's auburn hair and had inquired about the color of her dress, which she said was peach.

That night, when he handed her the box, she opened it just a little and peeked in, seeing a beautiful and delicate cream-colored orchid with earthy brown stamen and stripes set off perfectly by gold ribbons. She looked up at him.

"I've never seen a nicer orchid." She opened the box again—all the way this time, breathing in the fragrance. "Thank you, it's lovely."

He awkwardly took the box from her and lifted out the orchid, a ritual I've seen him do with her every Mother's Day, always chagrinned, always feeling that he wasn't good at it, always afraid that he'd hurt her. I suspect that he felt the same way on this first occasion. He retrieved the orchid's two long pearl-topped pins from the box. He leaned toward her but he couldn't figure out where to attach it—on the bodice or the shoulder. She slipped her hand under the fabric to show the way as he guided the pin in and back out again. And later, when my father danced with her, he did so with utmost care, making sure he never bumped into either the orchid or her breasts. He took every tentative step gracefully.

Charles and Alice began a ritual that night that lasted over forty years: they danced nearly every dance together. On the porch back at the house, he boosted her up onto the swing. They talked about nothing, enjoying the sound of each other's voices, and laughed. Charles reached up for her, and placing his fingertips behind her head, he drew her closer to him, carefully leaning in to kiss her.

"*I couldn't quite do it,*" he told his journal, "*so I planted one on her forehead.*"

At well past midnight when they said goodnight, the orchid's delicate white petals were so pristine that she wore the corsage to church the next day.

1975

"I liked that Charles right from the start," Grandma Bata told me while we sat across from each other at her little round lace-covered table near her living room window the year I graduated from high school. She insisted, even as we watched the marriage wound them, that their courtship was a love story.

"I set a pie aside every week just for Charles. His mother only made pies at the holidays," she bragged.

Bata baked pies even after they no longer needed to sell them on the street corner—as a way to love us. And as she saw Charles and Alice looking into each other's eyes and heard their full-bodied laughter, she told herself to relax. "God's looking after them—they'll be alright." On prom night, before she went to bed, she heard the porch swing creak. "Before heading up the stairs to bed, I turned out the porch light so they could have some privacy."

It was a simple gesture, which my mother learned from her. When a boy took me out on a date, our front porch light was on when he arrived and off when he escorted me home. Without knowing it, every eager young boyfriend I ever had should thank Grandma Bata for the cover of darkness. I will thank her for the pies.

Twenty years later, my piled-high glazed strawberry pie with whipped cream was a big hit on my date night with the "divorce recovery guy," who patched up my sexual self-esteem but nothing more. The next morning I faced a shame hangover that was not relieved by eating the rest of the pie. My ex-husband had provided me with seventeen married years, and he had at least seventeen complaints to justify his leaving. I knew them by heart and repeated them too often. What had I known about love? What looked like a marriage to me had apparently been a shell game. But I hadn't figured that out yet.

Chapter 4

The Porch Swing

I became more and more skeptical about love during my high school years. In the 1970s, even sappy movies about love had tragic endings. Take *Love Story* for instance—when the heroine dies, they don't live happily ever after. As the free love movement dawned on my generation, women claimed their right to independence. Girls who still believed in fairy tales were considered stupid and naïve. No educated woman in her right mind would give up her goals of an influential career only to be tied down to a husband and an infant, as Shakespeare said, "mewling and puking" in her arms. I had grander goals, and by the age of seventeen had fully dedicated my life to the church and developed a relationship with Jesus.

The only women I knew who got paid for working at churches were single women with schoolmarm sex appeal. The head of our education program at church, Miss Wyeth, had prematurely gray hair and pasty skin to match. She dressed in clothing reminiscent of *Little House on the Prairie,* worn with a Christian smile. Even when the kids knocked over a rolling bulletin board, sending her felted paper dolls of Jesus and the disciples flying across the floor, she kept her cool. Miss Wyeth's demeanor convinced us that she did not think about sex, ever. (Though for all I know she had a lover of

the same or other gender hidden away somewhere.) I met two female
Presbyterian ministers at a youth rally, and they were both single. It
just looked like that's the way I was heading. When I took off for
seminary, I was not going to find a pastor to marry—I was going to
become the pastor. It was a good fit for me since we didn't talk about
sex at home, and the church didn't talk about it either.

Falling in love was not on *my* to-do list, as it was for my parents
when they met. My father's journal recorded their naïve and hope-
filled journey into pheromones, hormones and the terror of love.

Every Saturday night from the first November snowfall through
winter and into spring, Charles drove his dad's new Chevrolet coupe
over to Alice's to pick her up for a date. Driving it made him nervous. He dreaded the look he'd see on his dad's face if he got even
one nick on the door's shiny finish or mud on the tires. A scratched
side panel would have sent his father through the roof. "I'd never
hear the end of it," he told Alice.

On a balmy night in May, they backed out of her driveway. He
started to put his arm around her and then pulled it back to insure
undistracted driving. She understood his message and snuggled her
hips next to his. They were headed to the ballroom of the Neil House
Hotel. Arriving early, they took advantage of free lessons. Alice was
unselfconsciously graceful. Charles' arms and legs hung loosely on
his lanky 6'2" frame, though, and the instructor often approached
with a frown on his face to help Charles coax his limbs into place.

"Take charge of those arms," the instructor barked. "Extend
them and use them . . . and don't be afraid to tell her where to go!
Remember to lead."

Once they mastered the basics, they were encouraged to mingle
with others throughout the evening to hone their skills. Following
the instructor's suggestions, they danced with various unpleasant and
awkward partners for a few weeks, but by the middle of winter,
Charles stopped asking other women to dance, and Alice declined
invitations. Only a few brave men cut in for a spin with her. And,
when they did, she returned to Charles' side when the song ended.
By spring, he stopped quivering when he held the small of Alice's
back. He gazed at the corners of her eyes when she smiled, taking
her in with a portrait painter's curiosity.

They mastered the waltz, the fox trot, and the two-step, and gradually became brave enough to walk onto the floor and start a dance. People around them paused and watched them in the center of the room, sensing the intimate connection they were forging. Charles felt gradually at ease with Alice in his arms. After they stayed until the very last note of the very last song, they still wished the night were longer.

The malted milk shop had red leather booths along a front window overlooking High Street. Famished by a full night of dancing, they tucked into the one they called "our" booth for burgers and conversation.

The waitress yelled, "The usual?" from across the counter and came over with two combination plates and sodas. Charles commented that the Guy Lombardo band was the "worst band I've danced to," and they laughed about how hard it had been to keep up.

Finishing her burger, Alice suggested they split a slice of chocolate meringue pie, the only pie Bata never made. He ordered one piece with two forks.

"You're a bad influence on me."

"Yes, I guess I am."

"Funny, how I like the influence, though."

He left the last bite of pie for Alice and then tipped the waitress generously. Around one in the morning, as he drove her home, High Street was still awake with trolleys and people cleaning up from the day's work. On Neil Avenue, they passed a group of frat boys making a ruckus. The fraternity next door played music so loudly they could hear it in the car. He whisked her out of the seat to dance with him in the driveway for a while, and then in a pause that demanded either a kiss or a change of venue, he walked her to the porch.

After the date, he wrote in his journal:

Alice started singing the first verse to "Fools Rush In" and I finished the second verse. She sort of laughed and asked, "Are we fools?" I wonder how she meant it. Later I asked whether we were going steady.

"I don't know, are we?"

"I kinda thought we were," I said.

"Rather!"
Later, when we kissed I said, "You're so very sweet."
We had a lovely, lovely night.

After their evening spent twirling around the dance floor, Alice studied for her classes in the downstairs parlor rather than her upstairs room, so she'd be close to the phone when it rang. Charles grew irritable when he couldn't reach her or hadn't talked to her in a while. Escaping his lonely life at home, he made up excuses to drop by Alice's, and Bata welcomed him with her outstretched arms and maternal hugs. In quiet moments of waiting for Alice, who was primping up in her room, his pulse slowed down and he relaxed. He was comfortable in this house, and though he didn't know how to put words to it, he experienced unconditional acceptance for the first time in his life.

A few weeks later, Charles ran up the porch steps at Alice's house waving his acceptance letter to Ohio State University like a flag in his right hand. Passing through the parlor to the kitchen, he was almost giddy.

"Hey, ho, anybody home?"

"Can I get you something to eat?" Bata caught him in the hallway.

"Not now, thanks. Go on, read it!"

"This is wonderful news, Charles. Congratulations!"

"Is Alice around?"

"No, I'm sorry, she went to a matinee with friends. She'll be so happy for you."

"Okay, I'm off to stand in the registration line."

He waited in that line for several hours, wishing he'd taken Bata up on the sandwich she'd offered. He chose late morning and after-noon classes since he wasn't a morning person, and he got on the wait list for favorite theater and fine arts courses. He passed the display for Delta Chi fraternity on his way out, and since his older brother had joined, he grabbed a brochure. The fraternity boasted a commitment to the great advantages, "derived from a brotherhood of college and university men, appreciating that close association may promote friendship, develop character, advance justice, and assist in the acquisition of a sound education." It would also bring him into close association with men and feelings he had not anticipated.

The fall of his freshman year, Charles fully took over the bedroom he and his brother once shared prior to Donald's graduation and enlistment. On one wall he'd put up an easel and stacked up wooden egg crates beside it with two tin cans full of brushes, one for the fine-tipped watercolor brushes on loan from his mother and one for the squared off stiff-bristled brushes needed for oil painting. The room was lit by a dormer, and standing there when the sun streamed in, he imagined himself an artist wearing a French beret—looking as handsome as Claude Monet in his self-portrait.

He pulled a stylus pen from his desk to finish drawing a nude woman, working quickly and not bothering with the details. Ink bottles cluttered the blotter, and he was pleased with his pen assortment, art gum erasers, and inks. Opening his sketchbook and grabbing an ordinary pen, he paused for a moment, imagining the painting of Michelangelo's *David* that he had seen on a plate glass slide in art history class. He pushed that thought and the journal aside and conjured up a young female art model with her arm draped casually across her pubic area. He sketched a chair in the center of the paper, and then, starting at the curve of the model's torso, he traced the line of her legs, leaving her hands and feet to be dealt with later.

Picking up his journal again, he wrote about his shyness around women. He turned off his light, and slept.

The next night, his entry read:

It has really gotten around the frat houses about Alice and me going steady. They said we were practically married and they talked about Alice as "your wife." They all seemed to think I'm crazy to go steady but some of them have gone steady in their time. I'm not hitching but I haven't found anyone as lovely as Alice. When I kissed Alice goodnight there were things running through my mind, things of how I adored her, loved her, but I couldn't get enough nerve to say it. Darn!

Parents are old as soon as you know them, and since mine seemed ever so wise, I have a hard time putting myself back in their naïve dancing shoes. Dad wrote words like "darn!" and "swell" in his journals. He thought he was a terrible driver and drove anxiously his whole life. (He later refused to teach either of his daughters how to drive and gave the job to Mom). By the time I was old enough to notice my father around the house, he was always covered with clothing from head to toe. Caught in his white cotton shorts after a shower, he crossed his arms over his privates, turned beet red, and skittishly ran for his robe.

He drank to manage his stress at social events. He wouldn't tell a joke at a party unless Mother was at his side. Then he played Gracie to Mother's George Burns, offering a naïve question that prompted an exuberant and dumbfounded response. He knew when to stop drinking in order to keep his emotions in check.

Reading his journal entries shifted my viewpoint—in the middle of a dance floor or on stage in a theater, he was no longer restrained. He played parts that were flamboyant, cocky, haughty, arrogant, and outraged. And with Alice, he was just a kid trying to find love in all the ways he'd been taught to do it. He bought the corsage, paid for everything, drove a nice car. He lived by his mother's adage, "If you don't have something nice to say, don't say anything at all," and was more content listening than talking. He liked holding Alice's hand and kissing her.

Alice, dying of cancer in her early sixties, sat with me on the lime green couch by the picture window and told me that these dancing years, these porch-swinging years, were their "best" years. And we laughed together about the nights they'd come home from dance club and dance around the living room. As a teenager, I'd sneak to the top stair to watch them down the hallway, and it reassured me to see them happy. They never stopped dancing together. Recalling these early years kept her in their marriage like a frame around a picture. She kept Dad's courtship journal because it made her smile and weep. And whenever she wanted to, she could return to being twenty again and remember why she fell in love with him.

Chapter 5

Awestruck

Courtship awakens nearly a dozen enervating biochemicals in the human brain, including feelings of elation, awe, closeness, trust, and arousal. Spend a few hours sharing intimacy-building questions with a prospective partner, and you will have the experience of falling in love. Biologists suggest pair bonding's inevitability. Despite my lack of any overt interest in marriage at age twenty-two, during graduate school I found a sexually liberated, charming seminarian, and we got married in Columbus, Ohio—on the day of the Ohio State vs. Michigan football game. When we set the date, Father protested but soon relented, and then spent a few months apologizing to his friends for our callousness. During the service, Don, Jim, and Ruddy had transistor radios in their pockets and wore earphones, occasionally bursting out "Yeah!" and "Go, go!" during the ceremony. We were thusly cheered on at the beginning of our seventeen years. I was as blindly in love as my young parents had been.

1939

While a nagging voice in Charles' head guided his attraction to men, an opposite voice, with growing volume, set him straight. His attraction to Alice came from his heart. He could have been thusly drawn to a newly discovered sister—she felt remarkably like family. Charles and Alice spoke often and privately about subjects no one had discussed with them before. Cherishing connection and deepening trust, Charles pursued Alice with the full intention to mate for life.

In her sixties, Mother said that their story would have ended differently if Johnny had driven up to her house in a brand-new Chevy and taken her to the malted milk shop for one shake with two straws and offered her some slick lines about her auburn hair or the maple syrup color of her eyes, and apologized for his insults and ruining the pie. But unlike silly girls, underneath her laughter and lightheartedness, she had a skeptic's keen wariness about men that most women didn't develop until three decades later. With Bata's enthusiastic belief in how smart and capable she was, she wouldn't easily be bowled over.

1962

I got a new glittery blue "big girl" bike the summer before the fifth grade and rode it the two long blocks up the street to my school. On the way home, three older boys chased me and then maliciously stopped and positioned their bikes so I couldn't go anywhere to get away from them.

"Great new bike," the meanest boy said, "but it's so shiny it needs a few scratches, don't you think?"

His friends agreed. They pulled me off the seat and bent the front rim, scratched the paint with rocks and took off. I couldn't even ride it home, and, when Mom saw me heading toward the house pushing my wobbling bicycle, she scooped me in her arms and let me cry a long while.

"Now, I'll tell you what. I'm going to go to those boys' houses and have a little talk with their parents. I expect them to apologize to you and pay to get your bike good as new."

Over the weekend she followed through, and every day for a month she met me after school and drove alongside me as I rode my bike home. My sister and I knew that Mother had our backs when danger threatened, which helps me understand her choice in marrying and staying with our father. She held her own.

She didn't need machismo in a man, and she wouldn't have tolerated any man with even a hint of violence in him. She detested overblown egos and would have kept her distance from men who were too hasty in love or too hungry to have her. She would have found any man's overly eager hand slipping down from her shoulder onto the soft cotton of her sweater disgusting rather than charming. She was looking for a gentler soul, a man of wisdom and manners, both of which my father had.

On a Sunday walk from church, Alice and Bata fell silent until Alice spoke.

"I guess I'll stick to Mr. McClintock." She was relieved to be talking honestly to her mother again. They were both falling for Charles.

"He's got more in his little finger than Johnny has all over," Bata said.

Charles had been complimenting Bata, laughing at her jokes, telling her how impressed he was by the way she could win a bridge hand while keeping up a lively conversation at the table. She grew to adore him. Years later, after Grandpa Sam died, she spent Sunday afternoons in our home at Dad's request. Mother kept her occupied with cooking and card games. Bata and Mac held on to a fondness for each other that slipped away from the rest of us.

2005

I sometimes go back to the question of how they decided on each other, and why, when both of them had other options. A Hindu cab driver from Bombay India educated me on this point while taking the long route from the Philadelphia airport to drop me off at St. Rafaela's Retreat Center for a writer's get-away. He informed me professorially that the God of the universe sets up the mood and the energy for the parents to have intercourse in order to produce offspring who would be born at the proper moment nine months later. He thus presented a Hindi version of Mother's beliefs in predestination. The hour, date, and month of the birth determine the child's personality, he said, so my mother's astrological sign indicated that she should partner with a husband who was born only under my father's agreeable opposite astrological sign. The stars' alignment would ensure a happy life. Without it, he predicted, they would have a life of pain, disagreement, upheaval, and suffering.

I wracked my brain to assist him with his analysis, but I couldn't recall their birth years to help him delve further into their astrological signs. I'm not knocking his theory or ancient wisdom. New biological research tells us that people pick partners for genetic improvements in the species. So perhaps their coming together had absolutely nothing to do with sexual arousal, attraction, or orientation. In my parents' generation, people paired up in high school and married quickly. They didn't have Dr. Phil explaining compatibility to them, an eHarmony website to help them match personality traits, or Dr. Ruth explaining the value of sexual awareness prior to marriage. My parents were young Presbyterians whose main mentor was John Calvin; initially they both believed that they were foreordained by God to meet and marry. Mother professed this to the very end. But other forces were working that she could never have anticipated or explained.

Over the years, I have had quite a discussion with this Presbyterian God as I try to make sense of this courtship and their later entrapment. Why would they be doomed to a disintegrating life? Did their weekends of dancing make up for Mom's celibacy and Dad's shame? Uncle Donald, who attended a strict Christian church that haughtily claimed to be the one and only, "THE Christian Church," believed that my father's misery was the result of playing cards and dancing. Donald fully believed and often professed to us that Satan enters the soul through these vices. He would, of course, have been absolutely terrified for his brother if he'd known of his sexual leanings. Presbyterians aren't Satan people. We don't expect little guys in red suits to send us to hell. Nope, we are slowly tortured by the God who planned out our misery ahead of time. And once misery hits, we just cope.

Mother considered her marriage an acceptance of her lot in life, the way she smoked cigarettes over the years and, when she couldn't quit, accepted her weakness as fate. After trying and failing several times, she shrugged it off.

"It's just a matter of time before I get lung cancer." She said this without remorse and kept on smoking.

I'm conjecturing here, but maybe the seeds of stoicism were planted during one of her college philosophy courses. As the professor lectured about the ability of people to carry on in the face of suffering, perhaps she filed his ideas away and later took stoicism on like a newly discovered religion. Once she had blended it with Presbyterianism, it came out something like this: "God made your bed and you lie down on it, so even if it isn't a bed of roses, all you can do is make the best of it."

Dad's journal notes show a more positive approach to pair bonding. He used the word *lovely* so many times that, as I typed them all into the computer, I thought it would start burning up pixels on my screen. At 19 he thought that life with Alice would always be lovely and uncomplicated. He was glad to have her near him, kind of awestruck about winning her heart despite well-hidden uncertainties. He quoted traditional wedding vows to her while he packed the trunk of the Chevy with her picnic basket for a day of fun at the river.

I want to reach back into their lives and stop them. Charles describes them merging into each other's worlds, talking easily for hours. He convinces Alice that life will be okay with him. He believes that they are meant to be, and how could I believe otherwise? When they are ready to stand before the minister who says, "If there is any reason why these two should not be joined in marriage, speak now or forever hold your peace," they don't know the pain that lies ahead for them. No one will raise a hand. My nineteen-year-old soon-to-be father doesn't analyze his sexual complexity on paper, nor can he see into the future. I keep looking to the stars for a deity who ordained it, and a philosophy to shed light on their unlikely connection, but I can't stop their courtship. It's definitely moving forward.

Chapter 6

Hamburg, Germany

I turned the page in my father's journal, and I virtually climbed into the rumble seat with them in the back of Pop's Chevrolet. We took off for picture shows at the State Theater across from Ohio State University. It was 1939, the year filmmakers describe as the greatest year in motion picture history. I was back in time with them taking in some fabulous films: *The Hunchback of Notre Dame, Gone with the Wind, The Wizard of Oz,* and *Wuthering Heights.* An amateur film critic, Father wrote descriptive paragraphs about each movie, including a film no one has ever heard about—a box office flop called *Confessions of a Nazi Spy* that starred Edward G. Robinson and a large cast of German actors. It wouldn't be long before my father faced the inevitable war in Europe that Hollywood scriptwriters and producers began depicting in films. But, for the moment, he was more interested in winning over Alice.

They were surrounded by gilded mirrors and velvet curtains, holding hands in the dark, laughing at the cowardly lion, sighing as Scarlett O'Hara stands proudly against the backdrop of her burning mansion. They were as naïve about love as they were about world politics.

A lifespan later, through the miracle of Internet search engines, copies of obituaries, and the Ohio State University archivist, I discovered that a lot more was going on that year. History revealed a young man named Walther, who would profoundly alter their relationship almost two decades after their first date. In 1939, he was across the seas in Germany at the start of the Holocaust, with no time to even think about love. He was painstakingly concealing his identity as a Jew and probably as a gay man. And while I step away from my job as narrator to lead you into Walther's story, I promise I will return and it will all fall together (or all fall apart depending on how we look at it) farther down the road.

Events on the world stage moved them all toward an unanticipated destiny.

Walther P. Michael, at twenty-six, was the youngest and most trusted employee of the L. Behrens & Sohne Bank in Hamburg. As was his daily routine, he arrived at the bank at dawn. On this clear Monday morning, while the March sun splashed the sky with faint red streaks, he told himself to act as if it were a normal day. He reached into his bulging pants pocket for a key ring. He briefly glanced down the street, and, as he opened the lock, he considered praying—but he hadn't prayed in a long while. He'd left his Evangelical Sunday School beliefs back in Freiburg, and he didn't dare consult the Exodus God his maternal grandparents believed in. He'd never felt so alone.

In his left hand he carried a small brown leather briefcase in which he had packed multiple documents showing that he had purchased his freedom by paying 90% of everything he had to the Nazi party. The process had taken months, and even now the chances were high that he would not be a free man at day's end.

He pulled the door shut behind him and locked it from the inside. The bank had been closed for nearly a year, its assets seized by party officials. Walther worked directly under bank president George E. Behrens, who was the fourth generation in his family to run the L. Behrens & Sohne Bank and international import/export business. Walther later listed this job on his résumé as "Junior Executive," though my father was the only one with whom he would talk about these years.

George Behrens was arrested after a pogrom in November 1938 and taken to Sachsenhausen concentration camp for nearly a year, leaving Walther the job of asset liquidation. Five years earlier, in March of 1933, Nazi party officials had begun removing the bank's Jewish board members, forbidding transactions with Jewish accounts, and seizing bank assets. Though some sympathetic leaders within the party protected banks and bankers for a few years, they could not stop the movement toward total Jewish extermination. Walther and others, including George Behrens, were classified as Jews under Nuremberg Laws, with wider and wider definitions for qualifying bloodlines moving them into higher and higher risk. After unspeakable horrors, upon his release, George promised Walther that he would find a way for him to emigrate, though it was increasingly dangerous to do so.

Walther walked through the lobby and entered the back office where he had worked for seven years. The bank had been shut down for the past year, and during the liquidation, Walther compiled lists, took inventories, and prepared to hand a four-generation legacy over to party officials. He set his worn leather briefcase on the countertop, thinking about the family pictures he had wanted to pack but left behind in his apartment—to be found and destroyed *like everything* he thought. He would soon be searched at checkpoints and several border crossings, so to avoid all suspicion he packed only what a man on a business trip needed for a few days: a change of clothes, a razor, and a handkerchief his grandmother had given him on the day he turned thirteen.

He opened the gold pocket watch he'd tucked into his vest pocket. His father had tearfully passed this watch to him on the day in 1933 when his parents fled to England. In order to safely keep it, Walther had found a sympathetic jeweler who rubbed out the inscription, helping him fade into anonymity under his English name. He continued to hide the fact that he had Jewish grandparents. His diplomatic skill, his ability to speak several languages, and his international connections made him useful to the Nazi Party. He checked the time.

He approached the bank vault one last time. With his hands slightly shaking from lack of breakfast and fear for his safety, he hoped he'd remember the combination correctly. Several small keys went into place and, breathing up from his toes to his lungs, he turned the latch. The door opened smoothly, and he stepped inside. Walther maneuvered a wooden crate onto a small dolly and wheeled it from the vault into the main office. He didn't take time to close the vault behind him. He checked his watch again, and now he had just five minutes to get the crate into the elevator and down to the back exit on the first floor.

He heard a distant door slam shut and felt his heart lurch into high gear and then settle itself again, as he identified that the noise came from next door rather than out front on the street. He would not have been surprised to find the front windows smashed yet again and a group of soldiers pointing guns at him. But this time, it was a false alarm. So he grabbed his case and called the elevator. He wrenched open its large metal doors and slowly pushed in the crate, stepped in behind it, and pushed the lever closed. It lurched downward and, at the basement level, he repeated the process in reverse.

He could see the car awaiting him behind the building. Its trunk was open, the driver acting nonchalant, though Walther could see the old man's face was tense and weary.

"Good morning, sir."

"And you, sir." Walther tipped his felted wool hat slightly.

"Let me help you with that." They both tipped the crate and carefully loaded it into the trunk. Walter sighed in relief that his measurements had been correct. He hastily stepped into the back seat, and the car sped off.

The crate contained a collection of art holdings from George Behrens's estate that he had placed in the bank vault, fearing his inevitable arrest. The paintings were bound for Belgium, and Walther went with them for nearly two hours by car, following the Elbe River's meandering path to the North Sea. That morning he had no idea what lay ahead, but he was determined to meet George at the harbor as planned. They would not shake hands or embrace, even though it would have been his inclination; even small gestures were seen as contamination between Jews and non-Jews. He would leave the pictures with George to secure for transport aboard ship. Walther reached into his overcoat, pulled out his ticket, and calmly walked away from George as if they had never met. He slipped in among the crowd on the gangplank and boarded the ship to Belgium.

Leaning his hands on the port railing, smelling rotting fish and the salty sea, he looked back on the homeland he loved. His thoughts went from Hamburg to his childhood in Freiburg and then to his mother and father in England—his eventual destination. He hadn't seen his parents since the family exodus began. Leaving Germany for what could be the last time felt like the second unbearable heartbreak. The day back in 1933 when his father called him home had been the first.

Walther had been puzzled by the urgency in his father's tone when he opened the telegram that prompted his visit. It said that he should come home to celebrate his mother's birthday on a date that was not her birthday. Should he read between the lines? Was she sick, or was his father? The train trip was uneventful, leaving his mind to wander over the beautiful fields and forests while worrying about the rising power of the Nazi Party. He looked forward to telling them all about his first-year apprenticeship in imports and exports at the L. Behrens and Sohnes bank in Hamburg. But there were things he wouldn't tell them about—threats to the bank and its Jewish patrons, or about his personal life.

Arriving at the house, he was reassured that all was well with them. A large floral bouquet in an antique porcelain vase adorned the entry table. The teakettle was boiling, and his mother had baked something sweet. She had a few more gray hairs but otherwise looked healthy. His brothers greeted him warmly and appeared well. The next morning they all attended church, and after lunch, she gathered them around her and ushered them into the formal parlor. Walther sat on a brocade settee next to his middle brother, Wolfgang, who bore his father's name but was not officially a "junior." Wolfgang was home from Berlin, where he was nearly finished earning an advanced degree in theater arts. His oldest brother, Franz, at 26, who had too much energy for sitting, stood behind the settee. Their father stood off to the side, leaning on the mantel railing over a fireplace they rarely used.

Surrounded by three highly intelligent men whom she loved more than her own life, Walther's mother took a deep breath, called up her courage, and began.

"I am not ashamed," Else Wehrenpfennig Michael said, looking at the floor.

Walther felt a chill in his soul as well as in the room. The cold in the town of Freiburg in Breisgau had not lifted in April 1933 at the Black Forest's westernmost edge. The room's ornate décor and Else's silk gown all reflected their status. His father's professorship had afforded them more than a comfortable life, and they valued education so highly that they had spared no expense in educating their sons.

His mother tried to make this gathering seem normal, as if it could be. She and the boys' father had carefully planned this occasion, knowing that their safety could no longer be guaranteed. The Nazi Party had arisen at a pace they had not foreseen. While Professor Wolfgang continued his teaching in the Germanic Studies department at the university in Freiburg, the rising prejudice and hatred toward any impurity crept silently into the national culture. And of late, the rising disdain and inevitable violence toward Jews, the disabled, blacks, and homosexuals in their beloved and bucolic land could no longer be ignored. She often felt powerless when Franz, still living at home, provided her with reports that a business had been taken, shop owner shot, a whole family imprisoned. When Franz (who was skilled in languages and had received top honors in law) accepted a position of attaché in the German Foreign Service, he was soon exposed to an evil of the sorts he had only read about in textbooks. She sometimes overheard him talking to his father late in the night and was both afraid to listen and too curious to ignore them. Protected by her gender from public discourse or power, she had grown increasingly suspicious, socially withdrawn, and emotionally distraught. Walther could see the weariness on her face that morning.

Walther watched his mother's eyes narrow in anger, or was it pain? He couldn't tell which.

"My dears," she was whispering so softly that Walther naturally uncrossed his legs and leaned toward her.

"We are Jewish."

Walther noticed that he'd forgotten to tie one shoe and leaned down to complete the task, not because he hadn't heard her, but because the adrenalin in his body had nowhere to go. He willed it into submission by simply taking one lace in his left hand, the other in his right hand, then slowly looping them around and pulling tight. He felt nauseous and in order to gain some equilibrium, he sat back up. He had never set foot in a Jewish temple. That morning he had gone with his mother and brothers where they all took communion at the wooden railing. Kneeling beside her, he looked up at the cross of Jesus at their Landeskirchen, the regional German Evangelical Church.

"Your grandparents, Oma and Opa, became Christians a few years ago, but their conversion does not matter to the Gestapo. They were born Jewish, and lived as Jews, so they are no longer worthy to hold property, work, or live freely. My lovely sons, you have Jewish blood, and I have 'contaminated' the family. We are all in peril."

"The party seized records from their temple," Wolfgang added, moving to stand nearer to her as tears overwhelmed her.

"We cannot reach them, and we do not know if they have gone underground to safety or been taken for deportation to a camp."

Franz leaned forward and put a firm hand on his brother's shoulders. Walther's hands had begun to shake.

"It will not be long before we will be counted among those with Jewish bloodlines, and your father's vocal sympathy for the plight of the Jews is known at the university." His mother shifted in her seat to discharge her anger and fear, looked briefly out the window, since seeing her sons in pain doubled her agony. Wolfgang drew near to her, squatted down, gently kissed her tear-washed face and then stood again.

"Your mother and I must pack our things this very night." His father's strong voice was reassuring. "A car will meet us before sunup to drive us to Vienna. There, we will board a train to Amsterdam and take passage to England. A colleague has prepared our papers for the journey under the ruse that I have been invited as guest lecturer at Oxford University and decided to take my family on holiday."

Franz stood nearly as tall as his father and, since he was at the invincible age, he dared to address him across the room more as equals than son to father. "Father, you won't be safe if I go with you. I know too much, and I am expected at work. My absence would be suspicious."

Walther stared blankly upward at Franz, watching his family breaking apart.

"Please don't worry about me. I have already planned my escape. I will make passage to China—and since I have mastered the language, it will be easy for me to disappear. I will go into exile for a while, until we are all safely settled."

His brother Wolfgang sagged in his seat and put his head in his hands. "I can't leave; I have to finish my program in Berlin; I . . . I think I'll be safe there for a while." He was desperately trying to put on a confident face for his mother's sake. Walther knew at that moment that his parents would have to take the trip alone. He was planning to return to Hamburg and continue to work as long as possible to protect bank assets and help other Jewish families. "I must return to Hamburg," was all he said.

Franz knelt down and hugged his sobbing mother while Walther rose to his feet. Franz then scooped Walther into his embrace. Walther clung tightly—feeling that his heart had stopped and if Franz let go, he would fall to the ground a dead man.

"I promise," Franz said, stepping back and looking Walther in the eye. "I promise to reunite us."

Leaving this grievous memory behind, Walther watched Germany fading in the distance and lingered on deck. The last postcard he'd received from Franz was stamped by the postmaster in Hangzhou, China, and pictured his office building at the Zhejiang University. Franz was planning to take a six-month visa to the United States. He didn't sign the card, but at the bottom he wrote, "I hope to see you soon!"

Walther pictured the postcard among the things he had left behind in his Hamburg apartment. He gazed around the deck for a place aboard the ship to sit for a while, the March wind growing stronger as they left the port. He breathed deeply, bone tired. His ticket had, blessedly, been checked and rechecked without much scrutiny. When he could no longer see even one speck on the shoreline, he took his soul, weary with grief and gratitude, and went below.

Chapter 7

The Radio Show

Throughout my childhood, between March and November every weekend day, my father abandoned us to tend gardens he had planted around the yard's perimeter. I recall the story in which Winnie-the-Pooh describes his frustrating relationship with Rabbit, who was always running off somewhere. Winnie-the-Pooh mused that it was hard to have a relationship with Rabbit's back end. In the Hebrew Scriptures, a similar dynamic troubles Moses' relationship with God. God only reveals His holy backside. I totally get it.

Standing on our back porch step, all we could see of Father was his backside. His baggy slacks and sturdy belt usually prevented an exposed butt crack, but not always. He wore a sleeveless white cotton t-shirt in humid warm summer months, and in the '70s he wore a do-rag to catch the sweat. Father had a relationship with his flowers that he didn't have with Mom, Marsha, or me. He knelt with them in meditation, laid them out like paint on canvas, happily anticipated their blooming, and protected them from invading bugs and weeds. When he couldn't be with them in down-pouring rain or snowy winter days, he spent his weekends "napping" up in bed. It wasn't until I read his journal accounts about his relationship with his father that I found the link to our multigenerational intimacy avoidance.

44

CLARA AND CHARLES MARVIN   CHESTER "CHET" McCLINTOCK

My father initially hoped that he could make his father proud. He could serve the country in war and get academic degrees, but he couldn't see himself owning or running his father's pharmacy business. The glad-handing required for sales, long weekend hours, and supervising nitwit teenagers didn't suit Charles. Accepting this about himself further alienated him from his father's affection. So he lived through characters in movies, reviewing hundreds of them in his journals. Going to "picture shows" gave him something to say when the family insisted on his presence in awkward social settings.

The distance between my father and his father began a generation before them. A porcelain figurine of Chet's parents leaning against a tree stump sat prominently on my mother's dresser. They appear stern and proper, but a careful observer could also see on their faces the tired expressions of immigrants newly arrived in the United States from Scotland with a handful of belongings and lingering dysentery. They came clutching a brown leather suitcase containing a quilt made by her mother, a few items of clothing, and the porcelain figurine, a wedding gift from James to Christiana. Chet's father lived only a dozen years after they settled in central Ohio. One winter day, as he collected coal that fell from train cars rumbling through town, he slipped on the tracks and was crushed to death by the train. Soon after, his mother was murdered by a man she refused to marry. Frightened and floundering, Chet's older sister married immediately and moved to a neighboring town. Chet, who was known for using mixed-up metaphors said, "She left before the ground froze over her own dear mother's grave."

Chet was left to raise three younger brothers. They survived by living under bridges, picking up newspaper delivery jobs, and stealing food. They all grew strong and did well for themselves in businesses, marriage, and the raising of children. He had cushioned the blow for his younger siblings with competency but not affection. I surmise that the experience permanently blocked his access to vulnerable emotions; while fearing loss, he withheld love.

One evening when Chet and Clara went out to dinner with friends, my father was alone at home. Listening to a Lux Radio production of *My Son, My Son,* he came to grips with his father's rejection. The story came from a novel by Howard Springs that was made into a movie. Two weeks before its release, an eighty-seven minute radio version performed by the actors was broadcast. Coincidentally, the story opened with a man reading his journal. It closed with these words: "I'm proud, I'm proud of my son."

Father's journal entry, March 11th, 1940:

> *This will sound silly, but I don't care. I cried tonight for the first time in many months. I guess I'm a victim of my emotions, but while listening to the play "My Son, My Son," over the radio this evening, I suddenly became aware of the realities about me. I know now, as I guess I have subconsciously known before, that my relationship with Dad isn't what it should be, should have been. We are as apart as night and day. Of course I get most of the material things I want, but the tangible things, the confidences, the binding love there should be between us is lacking. There isn't any. He lives for his work and that's all. I'm just the material result of his pleasure a long time ago. That's all.*

This sadness grew deeper as he contemplated his future.

I realized that I'm really just beginning my life and I've gotten off to such a bad start. I wonder if it will go on like this—always in a mess. Would it be better if God would take my life away before I make a worse mess of it and possibly make a mess of others, of those whom I may come to love? I don't want that to happen! Too many others have done just that. Oh God. I hope I don't make a failure of my life.

I go back to breathing slowly and consciously while I face the sober reality that suicide was a choice my father could very well have made. He seems to be writing in code about being gay and the shame this discovery could bring to the family. Like too many young gay men, he seems to have interpreted a life of radical difference as a messed up life, one not worth living. Had he taken his life, his family and friends would only have said that they never understood why he did it. "He seemed so happy," they'd have said. "He had everything going for him."

Charles fought his despair by going dancing with Alice. His parents barely even noticed his absence night after night. Alice's house was welcoming, lively, and busy—possibly the thing that kept him alive. At Alice's house he joked and laughed. About a month later, on Saturday April 20th, he wrote:

Well, I won the battle about joining a frat. Dad gave his consent this noon. Boy that's a relief. I hope it will be all I anticipate it to be. I've wanted it for so long and now that it is a realization, I'm a little bit afraid.

The fear was well founded. While rushing at the fraternity, he cavorted with fraternity brothers, learned to be sarcastic, told jokes that degraded women. They forced him into gross behaviors, fed him foods that made him vomit, and taught him to steal bras from the women's sorority next door. They blindfolded and urinated on him, they forced him to pick up peanuts with his butt cheeks, and they kept him up all night scrubbing floors. They plied him with liquor until he was sick and called him a girl when he showed emotions. He was sleep-deprived and harassed. And still he wanted their camaraderie.

On his final induction night, they announced the names of those who had passed with flying colors and then told him that they were sorry, but they had denied his membership. Then, watching the pain on his face, they told him they were just playing a prank. They mobbed him with punches and pats on the back and welcomed him in.

I remain curious about whether my father's fraternity brothers perceived his soft-spoken passivity to be gender non-conforming. Was he sexually attracted to them? Much of their activity together contained homo-erotic overtones, with nakedness and torture entwined in activities like sanding the floor in nothing but underwear. Denial may easily have been the emotional field in which he lived. In those rare moments when he talked to me as an adult, he described his own dawning awareness of being "different," all the while carefully avoiding the sexual orientation topic. "I'm not like other men," he said. "I hate the country club scene; I could never go out with golf buddies. I love art and flowers. I like my life among women at the office; I never know what to say when I'm with macho men."

Since gay men usually know about their "different" way of being as young as seven and usually by puberty, he could have carried secrets about his sexual interests for umpteen years. He avoided admitting this to himself, but hints show up in his writing. He describes himself at a dance on campus where he was the only one in a casual outfit. He wished it had been "louder" and that his uniqueness had been even more flamboyant. "I felt like a Hollywood movie star," he wrote of the night when he danced until midnight in his pleated pants and wingtip shoes.

If Chet and Clara had been more supportive and attuned parents, they could have helped their son accept his flamboyance. But that is an insight from the culture in which I now live, and many parents are still clueless about gender non-conformity. I can only read along in sympathy as my father Charles recorded his lonely search for acceptance.

Though his parents sensed something different about him, they couldn't have named that difference. Chet kept busy, avoiding sadness through achievement, and he left Clara to handle Charles-

Marvin's many moods. He never stopped to see the adolescent Mac, the sensitive creative young man, nor did he consider what his son might have needed. No wonder Charles finished writing about his relationship with his father by saying, "*I think that cordial is the best it's ever going to be. . . .*"

1987

On a visit home, mother handed me two tickets to Hawaii as a second honeymoon trip for my husband and me. Had I told her the marriage was suffering? By then her credo was staunchly my own: stay loyal to family secrets, and no matter what happens, never go back on a marriage promise. In truth, my husband and I were barely hanging on to the relationship. He had broken my trust, which we mended with thin threads in therapy, but we were still emotionally distant.

After serving separate small-town parishes for five years, my clergy husband and I moved with our five-year-old daughter, Megan, to the central valley in California to co-pastor a larger congregation. We faced multiple challenges in a conflicted church. The harder we worked, the less we saw of each other, and our home life became an extended staff meeting. We replicated the conflicts at work, and as my husband grew more rigid, I grew more controlling. Megan brightened our lives with giggles and smiles, charming us both with her winsome uncomplicated adoration. But we also needed time alone, so we placed her in good hands among church grandparents and boarded a plane for Molokai, hoping that the sun and the sand could draw us together again.

Watching sea turtles play in the waves near shore, I put down my novel and took in the salt air. Dwarfed by palm trees and distracted by the colors of blooming birds of paradise and away from ordinary tasks, I tried to conjure up loving feelings and send them over to the man next to me. With the warm sand comfortably baking my back, all I felt was intense loneliness. We hiked to waterfalls and ascended rocky cliff walls with gorgeous viewpoints, each step barely distracting me from the pain. On a mud-drenched trail in a rainforest, the path had been washed out along a sheer drop-off just ahead. My right foot slipped down the hillside and I collapsed into a squat, hoping that my trembling legs would hold me to the earth. Ahead on the path, my husband turned back to see me cowering rather than moving.

"Come on." He was more angry than concerned.

I yelled words that would make more sense years later.

"I will not go on!"

He neither coaxed nor pleaded.

"All right then, I'm going on without you—you can sit and wait until I come back or take the trail we came up. Your anxiety isn't going to stop me."

As I watched him go, I sat in vine-tangled muddy slime and wept.

And then the pattern showed itself.

Abandonment is a family trait. Great-Grandfather abandoned his son Chet by dying young, and Chet emotionally disappeared from his wife and his sons, Charles and Donald, in order to prosper, and passed the pattern to the next generation. My father abandoned his own identity and abandoned my mother with infidelity. I knew what I had to do—stop abandoning myself by tolerating secrets and lies. The insight got me up on my feet again and set my course back down the mountain.

Chapter 8

The Lesson

Alice could hear the disappointment in Charles' voice when she broke a date with him to go away for a weekend with her friend Jean. But Charles tried to keep his jealousy hidden. He didn't want Alice to know how much he relied on her to make him look good as they spun around the dance floor, and how his heart was healed when she listened to his frustrations with "Pop" while they ate burgers at the malt shop. The rushing process at the fraternity had not been easy for him; he was tired and he felt vulnerable. Still, *neediness is unmanly,* he told himself. He hoped that he had kept his annoyance about Alice's foray out of town from showing up in his tone of voice.

Charles' parents were also going out of town that weekend to a trade show for pharmacists. With not much homework to do and his weekend before him, he got a call from Tim Mullins. Tim worked with Chet in the back room of the Varsity Drug Store. He was a second cousin once removed, and Charles and "Timmy" met as children at a family picnic along the river. After high school, Tim entered the pharmacy program at OSU but never completed his certification. He knew plenty about filling glass pill bottles and using the Bromo-Seltzer dispenser in the shop. He was a good salesman, and he knew that for every ten-cent sale he made from the dispenser, eight cents stayed in the store and supported his salary. "Come on over to the counter," he'd say to a couple looking for a cure for gout. "You've got to try this—it stops the pain of headaches, calms your nerves, and settles your stomach. Once you try it, you'll want to buy a bottle to take home, too! It can cure almost anything." He frequently got the sale, which provided him with job security. Though Chet didn't give him pats on the back, he was trusted to run the store when the boss was away.

When the shop was empty, Tim stocked shelves with remedies—throat lozenges, iodine antiseptic, and Phillips Milk of Magnesia. In the window he placed the Whitman chocolates, Pond's beauty cream, and Phillip Morris cigarettes. And when he wasn't stocking or laying out displays, he read up on the war that was raging all over Europe. England was not yet close to defeating Hitler, and America was preparing for war. Chet had recently ordered a dozen eighteen-inch-high American flags on heavy stands, and before leaving for the night, Tim opened the box they came in. He took them to the front window, reached over the half wall, and randomly tucked three of them among the remedies and temptations.

Tim turned the sign on the front door from "open" to "closed" at around six that Friday evening and walked to a pay phone to place a call.

"Hey, Charles, it's Tim Mullins. Remember me? I haven't seen you stop by the pharmacy for your dad's car keys in a long time. Hear you're rushing for a fraternity. How's everything going for you?"

"Not too bad, and you?"

"Pretty darned well, thanks. I was thinking about that time our families got together for a picnic, what was it, ten years ago?

"I remember you'd forgotten your suit and just jumped off the rocks into the lake buck naked." Charles could still picture the scene quite vividly.

"Sun burned my ass off, as I recall."

After their laughter died down, the conversation briefly stopped. Grandpa Chet had asked Tim to go over and get Charles out of the house for "a decent meal" while they were out of town. "He can

mope around for hours," Chet had told him, leaving both the store
and his son to Tim's oversight.

"I heard you're an old bachelor like me this weekend, so how
about taking in a movie? Your dad says you're quite the movie critic,
and I haven't seen *Strike Up the Band* yet. Have you?"

"No, but . . . it's swell you asked. Only problem is I told Alice I'd
take her to see it next week." Cursing himself later in his journal he
wrote, "*I could have just seen the movie twice, damn it.*" He hastily
concocted another plan.

"Could you come over on Sunday? We can find something to
eat in this old refrigerator and then just go see what's playing. How
would that be?"

"I'll be there."

1986

Surrounded by pictures of Mother Mary on three walls, I uncom-
fortably slouched in a hard wooden desk chair made to fit fifteen-
year-olds in an adult class at a Catholic high school in Berkeley,
California. I was 36, but that likely doesn't matter. I was fidgeting.
I was listening with my eyes, watching an American Sign Language
instructor with her "f" hand shape flying, explaining that interpret-
ers often falter mid-sentence. When a language interpreter hears a
word that makes no sense in its current context, she says, the interpreter's brain shuts off all activity for a while. It's what psychologists
call cognitive dissonance. Walther and his brothers experienced this
brain shut off when they were told that they were Jewish. Whenever
the world turns out to be totally different from our expectations, the
shut-off valve protects us.

The middle finger on the interpreter's right hand passed across
her forehead in the sign that means nothing is going on in the brain.
Then she told the story of an inexperienced ASL interpreter who
was called upon to translate a lecture by a French cooking specialist entitled "The availability of mushrooms in Provence and their
influence on the local cuisine." The lecturer said that some of these
earthy fungi are quite "gay," and the interpreter signed the sentence
thinking that the word *gay* implied a lack of cross-pollination. She

missed entirely the speaker's tone and intention. He actually meant that these little mushrooms are happy and whimsical. Our teacher lowered her glasses and stared out at us. Then she signed, "The interpreter doesn't catch the word or phrase in its context, so her brain shuts off like an electrical overload switch that disrupts the current before a spark sets the house on fire." With her teeth clenched and a whooshing sound, her hands and arms burst into a swirl of flames. She said we could expect the brain to just shut down from time to time, and she finger-spelled the initials "GFI" and then "ground fault circuit interrupter."

Nearly twenty years later, sitting at my desk in a more comfortable chair, I was typing sentences from my father's journal into my computer. I yawned a bit and got a snack, bored by my father's detailed entries about picnics, nights of theater and dancing, and movie reviews. Dozens of movie reviews. They were all "swell" he said. His take on it all was consistent with stories mother told me about their courtship and early years. I sat back down and turned the page to find my father doing something far more provocative.

A journal entry from Sunday, October 13, 1940, read:

Tim Mullins came up this afternoon while I was working on a charcoal drawing for art class. We talked, smoked, told dirty jokes. Took him up to see what I had done so far in the drawing, then up to my room where we laid on the bed and talked of various things. Pulled down the blinds, undressed, played with each other's cocks and balls! He said he wondered what it was like to suck a cock. I said go ahead and suck mine if you want to. He said, "O.K . . . if you'll suck mine." It was agreed and he laid his head on my stomach and started sucking. I got no sensation but he liked it. I sucked his 8 and ½ inch cock (boy has it grown since the last time). It was sort of fun taking the big thing in my mouth and wrapping my tongue around it, etc. He got a sensation so he said and I didn't mind. He sucked at mine again and then jacked it off and I his. Dressed and he left. Hope he comes up to stay all night soon.

I leaned over the page, my brain in ground fault circuit overload. To be sure I had actually read this right; I pulled the page from the clear plastic sleeve I'd stored it in. It still said the same thing. Clear enough. The sign language teacher in Berkeley appeared in my mind, with her signs swooshing fire and the house burning down. I forced myself into a recently learned yoga breathing pattern: more breaths out than in. Two in, three out. Three in, four out. Five in, six out. Seven in, eight out. The adrenaline slowed, my hands stopped shaking. I rested them on my head while my thoughts unscrambled.

I didn't want my father's sexuality reduced to the spare description in his journal—bare hands on bare flesh. In this case the fellatio was so perfunctory, so banal. The shy and innocent man who was writing in his journal about being sweetly smitten by Eleanora and then Alice was also a normal, horny adolescent.

I took the journal to my women's writing group and they could see the pain that this scene had opened up in me, but they didn't understand my anger at his hiding this behind my mother's back. "Bravo," they said. "Good for him." "He got to explore his body like that." One of them even cheered him on with "Go, Charles!" My circuits were still overloaded.

For forty years, the Thornton Wilder play *Our Town* had been playing on the center stage in our family theater. All of the characters are sweet and in love with each other. All of them ache when one of them dies. They make the best of hard times and cheer on the young ones when they fall in love. Even with mounting evidence of my father's secret life and Mother's growing despondency, a part of me still lived in Grover's Corners.

After Tim Mullins, my view of my father as the leading straight man in our sweet Midwest post-war drama cracked apart. I was raised at a time when neither Hollywood nor Broadway portrayed sex like this. While the adult part of me was just fine with sexual diversity, inside I was reading his journal as an eight-year-old child again, idealizing him and fantasizing that I would find a prince charming just like my father.

As it turns out, I fell for gay men for a while. Roger the tap dancer from my ballet school had a lively flare, soft brown hair like my father's, and a laugh that drew me in. My flirtations ricocheted right off him. When romance and sex flourished among fellow counselors at a YMCA camp, I befriended a shy redhead with oversized dark-rimmed glasses—it frustratingly never went beyond hugs. Five years later at a camp counselors' reunion, he told the table group about his "newly" discovered gay sexual identity. I fell hard for a tenor in the college choir, an actor in the theater company, a guitarist with a sailboat who never laid a single hand on me even lying together in a tent watching the moon rise and the stars shoot across the night sky. I'd move closer; he'd move away. I just didn't get why it went like that quite frequently.

With his journal in my shaking hands, I asked my father out loud, "What am I supposed to make of this? How should I interpret this? I don't want to—you do it!" I hurriedly flipped back through the pages to revisit earlier scenes of romantic happiness. He had hoodwinked me again; see how he wrote that it was sweet and wonderful? I patted those pages with my hands, reassuring myself that for a while my parents were young and faithfully in love. They were Fred and Ginger, secure in each other's arms in perfect step with each other as Benny Goodman and his renowned orchestra kept the beat. I liked the idea that my parents fell into an ordinary, beautiful love. And I wanted their courtship to include infatuation and animal magnetism. As I sorted back through the journal for these scenes, I pulled out the picture of Alice and Mac on the front porch and set it up against my computer monitor as if to say, "Here are my parents in the lovely romance they said it was."

Like most people, I would have preferred our family to be inside the bell curve, to be normal. I wanted to hold on to my old belief that I had heterosexual parents who found sex together "lovely." Since I had a hunch that romantic sex wasn't going to connect them down the road, I wanted them to get off to a good start with a simple and uncomplicated love. I wanted my mother to experience a few uninterrupted years when my father's entire romantic and sexual desires were for her alone. I wanted his skin to be connected to her heart. At least in the beginning.

I stuffed the page back into its plastic sleeve and closed the journal. The intrusion of Tim Mullins was evidence of my father's infidelity, and I combusted knowing what lay ahead for him, and for the woman he chose to become my mother. Walking in a park alone, I said aloud, "Don't do this to her," and "Don't hurt her like that," and "Can't you see how bitter and sad she'll become?" I yelled at him in Heaven. "Come on back here and explain yourself!" And I cried a long while because my father, dead for 25 years, would not show up on demand.

The pain of any loss connects to the pain of every loss. Angry at Mother's innocence, I was angry at my own. I played her part in the drama. My marriage couldn't be mended with a romantic trip to the islands. The man I married had a hidden life I chose not to see, and, following her lead, I played my part so that everything was fine. Tim Mullins was only the first of a lifetime of relationships we didn't know about or pretended not to see.

I packed the journal into a plastic tub of old memorabilia and put it on the top shelf in the guest bedroom closet where I couldn't see it. True to our family culture regarding Dad's homosexuality, it was out of sight and out of mind.

And then, I let myself get angry.

My therapist told me that anger is a passion for justice gone awry. I may have looked okay to friends and family, but it wasn't going so well on the inside. Lying down on my yoga mat and breathing deeply, I would open my rib cage just far enough for the sobbing to come through. "What you don't know can hurt you!" I shouted to my silent departed father. "You left Mother in misery, and she roped me in to keep her company when she was lonely, and I hate you for that!" The pain that started in my father's childhood bedroom with two bunk beds, little lace curtains, and pages of art sketches, passed on over to my mother and then down to me. Self-righteousness is one of my strong suits, so I stayed with it.

Almost two years later, when I was finished with self-pity, I found compassion. My father never interpreted his life. It wasn't safe to. So he put his pencil to paper and wrote Tim Mullins onto the page as if he were making a line drawing of a nude in art class. No interpretation, only a representation. A museum curator at the Metropolitan Museum of Art, one of my father's favorite places in the world, said that the average amount of time a patron spends in front of a painting is three and one-half minutes. People gaze at the frame, read the blurb on the wall, look around the room, and then spend only one minute looking at the art itself. I forced myself to spend more than a minute looking at the art of my father with Tim Mullins.

I pulled the journal back out of the box, opened it up again, read through to the encounter with Tim, and sat back down at my desk to type it in, word for word. With more love than anger, I could now ask a whole slew of new questions. "Hey Dad, when did you know? When did you know men aroused you and that women, while very pleasant, were not heat provoking? When did you realize it wasn't working sexually with Mother? Who else did you have sex with all those years?" The more questions I asked, the more stifling was the silence.

At this point, I contacted the registrar at Ohio State University and began my search to find Duane, Dad's gay friend with whom I had dined over steaks and manhattans with my parents when I was in my early twenties. Duane, at six foot three, an inch taller than my father, had clear skin and a school-boy haircut. He was twenty years younger than Dad and worked under him in the office. He had an easy charm, and Dad was smitten by him when they met. They soon became a cross between father/son and friends. Duane introduced my father to the underground world of gay men on campus.

The current registrar found Duane's phone number for me and, with trepidation, I placed a call.

"Oh my gosh, Karen, I'm happy you found me," he said. I was relieved. "I'd been wondering how to find you and your sister since you probably got married and changed your names."

"We got married, but neither of us ever changed our last name. We're proud to be McClintocks."

"Your dad would be happy, too."

"Not likely, he wanted me to take my husband's name so that genealogists would know how to track our ancestry. And he didn't like hyphenated names either; they loused up the registrar's tracking system."

"Yes, I remember. He was a stickler about some things."

"Like spelling. He kept the letters I sent home, corrected the spelling of my words and gave them back to me on breaks. Well, anyway, how are you—are you still with Ron?"

"Yes, he's saved my life. We've made a nice home for ourselves on some acreage, we're content and still in love."

We had talked for more than an hour when I told him about the journal and Tim Mullins and feeling overwhelmed by all I wanted to know.

He said, "He's your father; you have a right to know *everything* about your father." I paused and fought back tears.

"Thank you, no one's ever given me permission to know much of anything about him," I said.

"Karen, I loved your father; he was a mentor and a friend, and I'll tell you anything I know."

"Can I call you again?" I asked.

"Yes, any time."

I contacted him a few times later to get identifying data about one of Dad's lovers, but we hit a roadblock. I knew I could call him after that, but his offer was like a restriction that once removed isn't as compelling—like my parents forbidding me to smoke pot and then, when I could, I still didn't. Duane told me that my father made a pass at him one time, the details of which I'm keeping private between them. He didn't say much about my father's relationships, or perhaps rightly protected their anonymity. We laughed together as he told me that he introduced my father to ethnic foods—watching his face turn red over hot spices in curry joints with psychedelic music. He clearly knew a father I didn't know, and it's liberating to know that if the mood strikes, I can still call him up and ask.

Growing up with a family secret, I had a hard time sorting out the difference between privacy and secrecy. As a pre-teen, I had been shocked that other kids knew so much about their parents' sex lives. Other moms and dads leaned against each other and then hurriedly headed up to the bedroom. Other kids overheard their parents' bed squeaking, or caught them in the shower together. I cannot remember a single time when Mother and Father closed, let alone locked, their bedroom door. They were that chaste. Every morning as Father left for work, he'd lean down and kiss my mother on the lips. Every evening he did the same when he came home, sometimes adding an embrace. Their hugs were like vitamins they took for better health, dispassionate but essential. When company came to the house, Dad offered Mother a peck on the cheek. Was this a ritual that supported their pretense, or an actual expression of bonding?

I never heard them in the throes of sex, but I stayed up late on dance club nights to secretly watch them from the upstairs hall. On those nights, they couldn't get enough of each other. They took off their coats, and he hung them in the hallway, and then he put a record on the stereo. He slid his arm around her waist and placed his large left palm against her back to spin her around. They took quick small steps around the living room to the sounds of a dance band—every bit as enchanting as Ginger and Fred on a night that was too young to call it quits. No wonder traditional Baptists claim that dancing leads to the sin of sex. For my parents it *was* sex.

My father, or perhaps I should say, the father I knew, was a man who was frightened by everything from stubbed toes, to overly hot days, to power outages in the winter. He was an overly careful man, and every night he put the contents of his pockets onto the top of his dresser in the same order—keys to the left, wallet to the right, handkerchief folded neatly at the back. He was self-contained and rarely spontaneous. But then, in his own words in a journal entry, he matter-of-factly described having sex with a man in the room where he and his brother Donald likely explored nothing more dangerous than pick-up sticks, comics, and model airplanes. My father had also just been inducted into Delta Chi fraternity through the portal of Hell Week. The sexualized, dehumanizing experiences they put him through are reminiscent of the humiliation endured by prisoners of war. Yet he reported them as coolly as a reporter in a war zone. His report about Tim Mullins reads like a movie director's script rather than a description of his feelings or passion from the inside out. He simply noted that sex with Tim "was sort of fun."

Somehow he tucked this experience away inside the carefully folded cotton handkerchief he put in his back pocket and went over to Alice's house a few days later. As I picture him at Grandma Bata's kitchen table, looking across at Alice over a warm apple pie, I am drawn back to Grover's Corners. It couldn't be more American, more normal, more of the perfect cover to throw over his terrifying, non-conforming desires. Nothing in the culture at the time helped him with the task of integration. *"I wonder if we will sit across from each other like this for the rest of our lives?"* he asked in his journal after his next date with Alice. My father had his "lesson," as he called it, with Tim, which may not have been the first, and he hopes for more of them, and then without more than a kiss to seal the deal, he married my mother. They spent the rest of their lives together, with less and less to talk about.

One month past his eighteenth birthday, when he was home alone, the doorbell rang, and it was Tim Mullins. They didn't call it sex. A few days later, he called Tim to come over to the house for another "session." I want him to forego this therapy, or education; it feels to me like he is betraying my mother because I am all too familiar with infidelity. He's heading them toward loyal but bitter lives. Duane told me on the phone, "Your mother always seemed so unhappy," as if a life without sex should have been okay with her. But my father is so young, I ache for him. He can't foresee that he is being initiated into a whole lifetime of gay sex and love. I wish he would have just kept that door closed, and that for Mother's sake and for mine, he had gallantly denied his desire and kept the promise he would soon make to her, "to be faithful unto death." I so liked living in Grover's Corners.

I look at the picture of them on her front porch again, and I notice that he's partially hidden behind her. I whisper to her, "Alice, he's hooking up with men on the side!" But I can see by her broad relaxed smile and the soft gaze of her mahogany eyes that she is completely caught in his spell. Her world felt safe in defined cultural categories, and no one back then had studied human sexuality through a different lens. It wasn't until the late '50s and early '60s when Alfred Kinsey, son of a preacher, grew tired of ignorance and blew apart the idea that sexual orientation is binary. Attraction, desire, and behavior all mix together, and none of them remains static across the lifespan. Instead, we all evolve into something beautifully more complex.

At the end of his life, when I was more certain of my father's homosexuality, I began to explore the hidden shame beneath the life he had lived. Did it begin with Grandma dressing him up, or with Tim, and did he experience remorse about one-night stands, brief flings, or bathroom sex? My mother's seething anger, which became more evident as their years progressed, would surely have exacerbated his guilt. As he looked at Mother across the kitchen table all those years, had he totally disappeared into a world of meaningless encounters? What could this have been like for him?

"It was hell," my father said. The muse standing in the doorway. "Just tell them that the shame was hell."

"Okay, Dad, I will."

SEPARATED BY WAR

CHARLES IN NEW YORK

Chapter 9

Pearl Harbor Day

As Nazi tanks rolled forward on the western front, they closed borders behind them. Walther and his brothers kept hope alive by envisioning themselves living safely among other European refugees in America. Walther's youngest brother, Wolfgang, an accomplished and qualified actor and director, was nevertheless denied the opportunity to work in the Deutsches Theater in Berlin in 1936. A travel visa secured his passage to Switzerland where he met and married his wife, Hadassah, who was from Philadelphia, and they moved to the United States in 1938.

That same year, Walther's brother Franz obtained a six-month transit visa to the United States. Two days before his visa expired, without a home to return to, he was offered a position as a research associate at Johns Hopkins University in Baltimore. He worked there from 1939 to 1942, while terrifying battles ravaged Europe, including the devastation of Poland, and the invasion of France. Airstrikes screamed terror across England for nearly eighteen months.

Walther lived a few months in England during this reign of terror, presumably visiting his parents. Franz fulfilled his pledge to reunite his brothers on safer soil by arranging Walther's passage to America on board the *President Roosevelt* from London. It arrived in New

York Harbor in the fall of 1939. In March 1941, nine months prior to Pearl Harbor, Walther went to a recruiting office to discuss ways his aptitude in multiple European languages could be put to use to end the Nazi scourge.

2010

On December nineteenth, the day after the nation repealed its seventeen-year ban on gays and lesbians in the military, I called my Ashland, Oregon, pastor. (I was no longer serving as a church pastor myself and ask you to be patient to learn more about that later in the book.) My colleague Pamela answered her cell phone, and I jumped right into the reason for my call.

"I'm wondering if we have time during prayer for me to talk about the end of the 'don't ask, don't tell' policy and my father's military service, since it's also near Pearl Harbor Day?" I asked.

Pamela listens for the Holy Spirit and isn't at all stingy or controlling about worship. She said, "Sure. Take as much time as you need."

The next day at church, she ushered me to a microphone so I could begin. "My father was a WWII military veteran. I have inherited his journal and will share a few excerpts with you. Some of you will also recall what you were doing on the day you learned about bombs dropping on Pearl Harbor."

Sunday December 7th, 1941

Today was a fateful one for the world and especially for us here in the United States. Today Japan declared war on us. And so it has finally come, that which I have feared, that which I had hoped and prayed would never befall us.

Alice and I were leaving the house to go to the White Christmas worship service at the university when a friend came up our walk and told us that Japan was bombing our positions in the Pacific. The mad cyclone was whirling ever closer and even faster toward us. The choir at the service sang Handel's Messiah. There was a message of peace on earth! Yet there is so little to be found now.

On the way back to the house we heard the awful thing on the radio that Japan had declared war on the U.S. I said, "Oh my God," and we were quiet. After we had pie at the Livingston's, I came home and listened to the reports as they came over the wires.

God only knows what the future will bring. . . . The draft age will probably be lowered soon. I have a feeling that I will be forcibly registering within the next month or so. All of our hopes of getting married seemed to be shattered. The possibility of my graduating is very slight.

I turned to the next page in his journal before continuing. The congregation was unusually still.

Monday, December 8, 1941

We all sat about the radio at the fraternity house this noon to listen to the fateful speech of the President. And I wondered how many of us who were there would live through this terrible thing that has come. There were grim faces. Some of the mothers came in for the Mothers' Club luncheon. What did they have in their minds? I wondered how many of us will die in the war. God only knows.

His mother was a member of that club and never missed a luncheon. Her plans for Charles came to a halt that day.

I told a friend that I would never consider marriage to Alice now. To have me at war and her back here going through hell worrying every day would be a sinful thing for a man to do to a woman.

He kept the *Columbus Journal* that he refers to next.

I bought a paper this afternoon from a dirty little blonde-haired boy who came into the drama studio. I wanted to save it. It said in big headlines, "US DECLARES WAR." As I walked up to the house for dinner this evening, I thought how unbelievable it was. It seemed so calm. There was light by the street lights. I wondered how soon we would be putting out those lights for blackouts. We had declared war; it seemed impossible. There was nothing to be excited about over that. But to think that we might be attacked, that our cities might be destroyed seemed so unusual. It may happen tomorrow, next week, or, maybe never. Time alone will tell.

The sanctuary took on the hush it has during funerals, without a song to help us move forward. I closed the journal and waited respectfully.

"Friends, I bring you this story, my father's story, for two reasons. First, to remind us that peace on earth is a fragile, precious thing. And now that our nation has overturned its discrimination policies in the military, I feel free to speak for the first time about my gay father who served his country well. I am prouder today than I have ever been, because at last the stigma and shame are lifted. Our soldiers are free to love whomever they love, and with equality and justice in place, peace is our witness to the world."

I sat back down in my usual spot in the congregation while Rev. Pamela offered prayer. After the service she invited me to stand next to her. A dozen people formed a line to talk to me.

The first woman leaned toward me and quietly said, "My gay son is in Iraq."

"My lesbian daughter is a lieutenant, and I'm so proud of her," the next man said.

"Thank you" and "Thank you," a dozen times.

"I'm gay, and you have honored me today as well."

Coming out proudly came out that day.

When I began searching for the gay father I thought I had but could not be sure about, two books influenced my evolution. The first was a book on children of alcoholics that I read searching for reasons behind my neuroses. Most of it fit, because secrets foster similar symptoms in families. We had don't ask, don't tell rules in our family. We couldn't talk about Dad's sexual attractions or behavior, but we also couldn't talk about anything close to subjects that would lead us to the truth. We also had rules about being nice, avoiding conflict, and staying hypervigilant to make sure that everyone was okay.

And then I turned to the largest book I have ever read, *Conduct Unbecoming: Gays and Lesbians in the U.S. Military,* by news reporter Randy Shilts, who died of AIDS at a sadly young age. I pored through the pages in record time, searching for my father in there. My pictures of him with his boot camp buddies—the ones he never talked about—made more sense. When Mother said, "You don't want to know that," to me after I asked who they were, she was protecting his honor. I give her credit for that, and it was fifty years later that I stood up in church and, in a very different way, did the same.

Chapter 10

Farewell

With a sigh of relief, Charles closed the mailbox and headed back into the house. It had been months since he filed papers for his deferment appeal. *"I just want to finish out my senior year, and so do all of the others,"* he wrote. As he watched fraternity brothers pack and leave each week, he recorded their names in his journal and said that he prayed for each of them, increasingly anxious about his own fate. *"This is a fateful day for the entire world."*

September leaves turned and fell; the holidays came and went, and the boarding house grew quieter, with some boarders having gone into the army. Charles lost his heart for school and did the minimum work required for decent grades. As the winter's cold settled in with snow piling higher, he gave up hope of deferment. When in February the draft board increased its registrations to more than 150,000 per day, he was among them. He walked across campus to the old armory and got in line behind about fifteen others. Uniformed officers approached him. "Step aside, son," a sergeant quipped, and Charles thought he was in trouble. "Relax," the officer said. "We're just moving you to the head of the line; there's a reporter here from the campus newspaper, and he wants to take some pictures while your father registers you."

Though he didn't show it, Chet was worried for his second son, who didn't seem like soldier material. He was his momma's helper and too soft to be safe on a battlefield. Chet hoped that Charles could become an officer and stay behind the line of fire.

Charles looked over the other recruits' heads and saw his father standing behind an eight-foot folding table volunteers used as a makeshift desk. The day before, Chet had told his supervisor at the registry board office that he wanted to be at the table when Charles came in, and they agreed.

"That's a great story, Chet; let's be sure we have a reporter over there tomorrow."

"Father Registers Son . . . ," *The Lantern* headline announced the following day. Chet reached across the table for a tentative handshake.

"Aww, come on," said the reporter. "You got to come around that table for the picture." There they stood, awkwardly arm in arm: Charles too apprehensive to smile or mug for the camera, and Chet, who almost never smiled, trying his best to look like a proud father.

At home, Chet demeaned his son's artwork and felt threatened by his close identification with his mother, telling Clara, "He's too happy and frivolous." Charles' only interest in his dad's hard-earned Varsity Drug Store was to drop by the lunch counter for a "Tan Cow" (my sister says Chet invented this variation on the Brown Cow soda)—Vernors ginger ale over vanilla ice cream. Charles had long ago told his father to stop hoping he'd ever want to inherit the drug store. Standing together on enlistment day, with the camera's public eye pointed at them, his usually dismissive father was acting like Father of the Year. Charles wasn't smiling.

The picture gained Chet some great publicity, which he craved. Chet was well known in the community as the head pharmacist at OSU and supervisor of Portal Men at the football stadium. He belonged to the Faculty Club, the University Business Officers Association, the State Pharmaceutical Association, and University Lodge No. 631. Standing alongside his son when the reporter's camera clicked, he had one more credential to make him look good.

But Charles was not caught up in the glory of it. The day before leaving for boot camp, he wrote in his journal, *"Today I lose my freedom—I become a cog in the machinery of war.*" He packed up his duffle bag for an unknown future, but he never mentioned the possibility of his own death, loss of limbs, or living in trenches. He didn't even say if this was a cause he could believe in. The war was out of step with his life of romance, acting, and card nights with other men at the fraternity house. He wanted that deferment desperately.

Just a little over a month after registration day, he peered into the mailbox and saw his induction notice. As if the letter were contaminated, he stepped back from the curb, kicked his foot in the dust, lowered the little metal flag on the box, and then reached in and pulled out the thin envelope. He opened it there on the street, walked into the house, headed to the kitchen, and yelled, "Mom!" only to hear it echo back to him. No one was home, and since his journal was always there, he pulled it out of the center desk drawer and sighed as he wrote, "*Luckily, they had an engagement elsewhere with friends.*" The silent house gave him time to collect himself.

An hour later, he drove Pop's car faster than usual to Alice's house. Grandma Bata met him at the door and, without even knowing that he had arrived with news, opened her arms to hug him. Alice knew from her first look at him exactly what he had come to say. He looked lost for a moment and then pulled a chair up closer to her, and they numbly stared at the letter. When he took her hands and she began to cry, he forced back his own tears. "*I can't stand it that she cries,*" he wrote later that night. They stayed up talking long after everyone in the house was asleep. It was a Saturday night, and he later confessed in his journal that they had skipped their usual Sunday morning worship service. He was too tired and too sad to attend. After a few hours of fitful sleep in their respective beds, they would meet and go to worship that evening—it was Christmas Eve.

Their usual happy moods were glum on Christmas morning, and they sleepwalked through family rituals. Alice gave Charles a black-and-white picture of herself that she had colorized, painting in the details of her brown eyes and pink lace collar. She placed it in a beautiful small leather case, and he said that, when he got it, "*It almost broke my heart.*" He would tuck it into the vest pocket of his uniform every day he was away from her.

For the first time in his life Charles felt deeply connected to someone, and as often happens, saying goodbye confirmed this. How could he get along without her? She had become his dearest friend and trusted advisor. They played together with easy laughter, saw the world from the same political viewpoints, and believed in God without futzing around with the details. He was shaky and unstable as he thought about taking off alone.

On Monday he finished his packing, while Alice and both their parents waited for him to appear in the parlor. Grandma Bata saw him in the doorway, reached over to hug him, and took a long while to let go. His mother wiped her tears with a fine lace handkerchief and whispered "Stay safe" in his ear. He swept Alice in his arms as if they were heading to the dance floor and, when some distance from the others, he kissed her softly. He took her face in his hands and memorized it, then kissed her again. She didn't cry, for his sake. He penned, "*I told Alice farewell; I didn't want to say goodbye.*"

Chapter 11

Boot Camp

As the Vietnam War escalated in the early '70s, college students around me were drafted and pulled off course to serve in a senseless war. I became vocally opposed to the draft, which did not go down well at home. Learning that I supported conscientious objectors, Mother quipped that a young man *should* enlist in the army because "It will help him grow up." It could also help him sort out his sexual leanings, but she didn't explain that. Mother said that Father "came back from the war a changed man," and that's as far as she went.

My father went off to boot camp in February of 1943. At that time in history, under the watch of senior officers, there wasn't much room for sexual expression. Historians describe most gay soldiers as painfully closeted, never admitting even to themselves that they were gay. Charles was suddenly in a world of men, for which he'd been ill prepared. He didn't want to be a closed-off man like Chet or compliant like his older brother, but he didn't know how to accept his uniqueness in a gender-role limited world. While drinking at the commissary or rabble rousing on the town, he had to learn what to do on the fly.

Officially, after the passage of the military's Separation Policy in 1942, he could have been prosecuted under articles of war for being homosexual or bisexual (even when celibate) and given what was called a "blue discharge," causing him to lose all veterans benefits. But since the Army needed every man they recruited, they weren't quick to move toward discharge. Soldiers caught in sexual situations were sent to sick bay to be examined by a psychiatrist who placed them on a list in one of two categories: "Experimenters" were deemed relatively harmless and returned to duty, and "confirmed perverts" were given shock treatments, drugs, or administrative discharges. The threat of punishment went a long way toward keeping Charles and other soldiers in his platoon from displaying anything that could appear sexually deviant, even as they longed for connection.

Charles took his requisition papers, overstuffed duffle bag, and Alice's picture aboard the westbound train for Ft. Benjamin in Lawrence, Indiana. Boot camp drills and fitness challenges, demanding officers, and mental humiliation followed for ten grueling weeks. He slept in a room resembling a chicken coop with rows of cots, where he compared himself with bunkmates, saying they were far readier than he for the soldier's life.

While he kept up his daily journal, he didn't have time or energy to write letters home to Alice until he moved to a base in San Antonio, where he said it would at least be sunny and warm.

Greetings from the San Antonio front! If my writing is worse than usual it's because my fingers are numb and shaking with the cold. They say it is about six degrees below zero here. I should guess it were worse. We've just finished drilling a few minutes ago; they only kept us outside a short while, but it seemed like hours. My greatest fear is a scheduled hike tomorrow. I think I can stand most any kind of weather, heat, rain, snow, but bitter cold is just too much!

A few weeks later his mother received this note:

After saying a half dozen times that I wished they'd get me out of here today, the good news arrived this afternoon—I had ten minutes to dress, pack, and check over all my field equipment and bed clothing. That was impossible. I shoved things in the barracks bags like mad. What a mess they will be in when I unpack them. They knew I

was to move all afternoon but they waited until the last minute to tell
me! But who cares when I am out of this town!

Charles was ready for freedom and liberation in New York City,
where a guy on leave could find a guy who wouldn't tell.

His superiors gave him a promotion and a top-secret job in the
underground bunkers in the harbor just south of the Statue of Liberty, where he watched radar screens for enemy U-boats and submarines. At night he explored the city. The Empire State Building, the
world's tallest building at that time, beckoned him to climb every
step to the top. He frequented the Metropolitan Museum of Art and
lingered with the impressionists. He gathered some buddies to walk
up to the USO, where soldiers could snag free movie tickets. To Alice
he wrote,

> *We stood in line about a half hour. It was worth it though since we*
> *saved quite a bit. We walked to the Strand Theater which is at Times*
> *Square. We saw* Casablanca, *also Sammy Kaye and his band: damn*
> *swell all around entertainment. Of course it sort of cuts me inside*
> *at times when situations become similar to yours and mine. After*
> *the show we went over to the Service Men's Center at Times Square.*
> *We got hamburgers for five cents and of course all the Pepsi Cola*
> *we wanted. The place is very modern with lounge chairs, etc. In the*
> *lower floor is a big room for writing letters and entertainment, toilet*
> *facilities including showers, shaving cream, powder, etc. One could*
> *almost live there!*

A week later, he carefully opened a dainty letter from his mother
and rubbed his fingers over the purple violets she had carefully
painted along the paper's scalloped edges. She said:

> *I was watering the violets in the front window when the carrier came*
> *along. He knows how I look for those letters from New York. He*
> *stooped a little and held out the letter from you so that I could see it,*
> *then, when I went to the door, he said, "I bet I'm welcome today, for*
> *I've got just what you're looking for." I should have started this let-*
> *ter out by saying, "Hi, Private First Class," but it's not too late now.*

Congratulations, big boy, you're stepping right along. Next thing you'll be telling me of being made corporal. That will come in due time, but I think you did well to be advanced so soon after starting your new work.

He tucked it into a small box in his foot locker at the end of his bed so he could pull it out easily and read it a few more times. He wasn't sure he'd make it to corporal or wanted to, but she'd patted him on the back with her words, and pleasing her felt good.

I imagine him lying on his back, in the room he shared with a dozen other soldiers. He put his hands behind his head and allowed himself to really look at the men around him. Some were undressing and heading for the showers. He heard two of them telling crude jokes, one of whom looked like Tim Mullins, so he switched off those memories to prevent an embarrassing erection. His arousal patterns confused him. He got out his pen and paper and wrote a letter to Alice, perhaps to reassure himself that he was a man with a girlfriend he planned to marry, only what he had to say wasn't particularly romantic.

Together we will fight this war to victory and we will have our happiness in the future life we share as one. When I feel I most want to talk things over with you, I realize we do not think alike on some things. I guess we seem more like brother and sister than one might think.

Reading this note, I couldn't help but wonder if he was sending her an unconscious message that they saw their relationship differently. Was he trying to ask, "What if I'm gay?" She had certainly become the sister he never had: loyal, compassionate, and supportive. He soon moved into an apartment of his own on the Upper West Side, a privilege he gained with his advancement to Private First Class. He wrote to her nearly every day.

My darling, you can rest assured that I am happy in my new surroundings. This is more like what I have been used to having. And I thank God that I am so free again. Of course, saying that I am happy can never be entirely true until I am with you again. My dearest, I

DONALD AND MARY HELLEN, ALICE AND CHARLES,
CHET AND CLARA IN NEW YORK

love you so very much. Everything I see reminds me of you and how I long to have you near me. Until that time comes, I'll send you a kiss through the air and hope you shall receive it with all the love that goes with it.

Good night my sweet, Marvin
P. S. Come and visit me, please.

Alice went to her boss the very next day and negotiated time off from work at the library. The family forbade her to travel alone, so she was accompanied by Clara and Chet. They boarded a train for Grand Central Station in the early spring. Alice grabbed the mail as she left home, threw it in her purse, and opened a letter from Marvin on the train.

My Dear Alice,

There's a nice little diner near the apartment building where I had lunch today. They give you plenty to eat and it's reasonable enough. As an added feature, ice cream is added to the pie, free of charge to men in uniform. Total cost for food today was a dollar forty. Supposedly I'm ahead ten cents today.

He promised to take her there for pie à la mode and a dime left over. "*I just need to relax and enjoy myself,*" he mused, anticipating their visit. It didn't make much difference in his level of dread. Clara and Chet were highly skilled at comparison shame, so he knew they'd go on and on about his older brother Donald's wonderful accomplishments. He simply had to tolerate them in order to be with Alice. He devised a strategy to keep them all busy. They took the Staten Island Ferry for snapshots of the Statue of Liberty. They walked across Central Park to visit the Metropolitan Museum of Art. He accomplished his goal—tiring out his parents so they'd turn in early, leaving him and Alice evenings alone. Mindful of his Cinderella, he returned her to her hotel before midnight.

On their last night, they lingered in the lobby as long as possible, drawing the attention of the desk clerk. "Hey, fella, you better let this lady get some rest," he said, winking. Charles pushed the elevator button and sent her to her room next to his parents and went home to his apartment, so lightheartedly that he nearly floated above the sidewalk, thinking he could enjoy his whole life with her. Seeing them off at the station the next morning, Charles held her closely and inhaled the scent of Evening in Paris, a fragrance he'd chosen for her. She squeezed his hand and promised to keep writing. So he was not surprised to get a love note soon thereafter. She wrote:

Naturally anyone I see asks if I had a good time in New York and I have said "Yes" with explanations, so many times that I'm considering making a sign to hang around my neck. Now it all seems like some lovely dream I had, if I could only go on dreaming it.

She was obviously smitten, but while he played a love-struck Romeo, he also knew that tragedy would befall them if his attractions to men were known. A subsequent letter from her was not reassuring.

> *Hello dear heart,*
>
> *I feel I should scratch a line to you and sort of apologize for the wonderful time I had at the Navy U. S. O. event this afternoon. The tea dance was a definite success from my point of view. In the scramble I drew a fellow named Hayden Jernigan from Texas. He was a rather femme fellow at first, but you soon forgot about that when he started to talk. I seem to run to type. He graduated from the University of Oklahoma with a fine arts degree and was working as an interior decorator when he joined the Navy. He enlisted and came up the ranks and declared that he was glad to say that they hadn't just handed him a commission. He was a wonderful dancer and we got along fine.*

Here lay evidence of mother's skill at selective knowledge. She seems comfortable comparing the "femme" fellow she has just met to her sweetheart Charles. Had she hoped to open a dialogue about this trait? Did she hope to strengthen his resolve to marry her before she found someone else? To finish the letter, she went back to romantic illusions.

> *Toward the end we all gathered around the piano and sang. Fannie Straight was there and sang "When you're away." When she had finished, one of the girls really went to pieces. The tears just rolled. And the rest of us joined her.*
>
> *I'm thinking of you with all my heart,*
> *Love, Alice*

He scrutinized the letter. *What had she meant by the "femme type"?* He didn't want to be a "type," and "femme" just didn't sound good coming from her. A rush of adrenalin coursed through him, and he recognized an anger he usually reserved for his father. Would she dance with Hayden Jernigan at the next USO dance? Could he offer her a family fortune in oil or cattle or commodities—damn it, whatever they have to offer in Texas? *Maybe I should be dancing with him,* he might have laughed sarcastically, avoiding his fears. But since he didn't like to feel anger with himself and especially not with her, he tucked the letter away.

Before writing back to her on a lonely Friday night, he opened a can of soup, ate Premium Saltines from a tall tin, killed two cockroaches, and tallied their demise on the wall above the sink. No matter how meticulous he was, compulsively cleaning all two feet of countertop after every crumb, the invaders still scurried around the apartment relentlessly. The body count had reached seventy-eight.

He pulled out paper, the stylus pens, and an ink jar from a wooden box above a desk he'd made with two-by-fours and metal pipe legs. He pictured her with her shoes off, reading, draped easily across her bed in her attic room in the Waldeck Avenue house. He couldn't talk about the submarines he'd spotted nearing Manhattan that day or the fear he'd grown accustomed to. Sometimes he also feared that she would find someone else while he was away, and when this fear arose, he composed prose poems and mailed them to her the next day.

"*I pray that we will have a life of love we so deeply yearn for. I pray that we will be able to marry soon, I pray that the war will be over soon and I can be back in your arms.*" Living in a city alive with art and culture, he both longed for home and shamed himself for having such an easy deployment. He told her, "*If it weren't for this damned right eye I could have aimed and shot a few Krauts,*" he cursed. "*I'm not marching through mud or digging a trench.*" From time to time he'd get word about a friend who came home injured or won medals for carrying wounded bodies to safety. Several fraternity brothers died on the battlefield. He tried to imagine the raw courage it took to cross a field under enemy fire.

"*There's no such thing as a good war,*" he wrote on a single journal page, and then he turned to the next one and kept his pen flowing. He didn't recognize God anymore, he wrote, at least not the God he'd heard about while sitting in the pew next to his German mother. "*I haven't told anyone that my mother is German. Her God allows evil so that He can be glorified; what kind of God is that?*

Only a vengeful God takes young children and gasses them, hauls homosexuals off to die in work camps."

He paused, wondering if his mother ever questioned God's condemnation of homosexuality as he did. And then he wrote directly to God, *"Give me something new to work with."*

Reading through these notations, I am startled that he even knew about the German persecution of homosexuals. While fifty thousand suspected homosexuals were imprisoned in Germany during the war, this was a well-kept secret, and these prisoners were not acknowledged as victims of the war until decades after it was over. In concentration camps, up to fifteen thousand Jewish homosexuals along with non-Jewish homosexuals were forced to wear pink triangles for easy identification and targeting. They faced castration, hard labor in work parties, and death by beatings, but this was not generally described in the media. How did he know to rage against this injustice? My questions are stacked higher than his answers.

If my father's coming out process follows a common trajectory, he likely explored underground news sources looking to find his identity. He also prayed to overcome his shameful condition and asked to be freed from what he referred to as his *"nuisance."* And he thought, like others, that the best way to deal with his homosexual fantasies was to turn his thoughts toward a happy future with Alice.

He hadn't seen Alice since she had visited in the early spring, so he had time to save what he always called his "hard-earned cash." He began his four-day leave the following October, with a visit to a jewelry store in the heart of Times Square, where he bought a traditional cut diamond in white gold with three small stones on each side. Walking back to his room, he thought about buying a little brick house, raising children—an idyllic future with Alice. He imagined the life young men in that era dreamt about, the one prescribed for him by every film he watched, every love song on the radio, the future his mother wanted for him. He was ready to do what a man was supposed to do. He found a kind-hearted woman and secured her with promises and prayers.

"Something came in the mail for you, Alice," Bata teased as she called out through the screen door. Charles had arrived on an earlier train than predicted and was standing in the living room with a small and very promising box in his hands. Up the porch steps she flew and saw him through the door, arms outstretched. Books thrown aside, they twirled around in a grand hug.

"Look how handsome you are in that new uniform." Alice stood back, beaming.

"Sam," Bata hollered up the stairs, "get your head out of the newspaper and join us down here."

Grandpa Sam was a little like Fred Mertz from *I Love Lucy*: lovable, but clueless. As usual, he followed his wife's command. Now arm-in-arm facing each other, Charles wasted no time. He knelt down on one knee and passed her the box. "Alice, will you marry me?" His boyish dimple-cheeked grin said the rest.

"Yes—of course, you silly," she said, and set the unopened box on the table. She took his arms and raised him back up to his full height, clutched his collar to draw him near, and kissed him.

Bata pulled out the chairs around the dining table so they could all sit down. Alice put her right knee on the chair but remained standing to be near to Charles. She reached for the white felt jewelry box, removed the string, ripped back the brown paper covering, and opened the hinge. Sam let out an admiring whistle. She passed it to Bata.

"Lovely," she said, and because she was too choked up to say more, she passed it back.

"Well—try it on," Sam urged Alice. It slipped on a bit too easily. Bata could see Charles' worried brow.

"That's not a problem. I know a jeweler who can size it down for us."

Alice stretched out her hand and admired it. Then she hugged Charles the longest, but each parent as well, slowly moving around the table, feeling a little wobbly kneed, knowing that she'd be leaving this home she'd loved, while being very joyful at the same time. When she finished hugging her mother, she looked up to find everyone in tears.

Chapter 12

Engagement Letter

That night, Clara and Chet joined Bata and Sam, Alice, Charles, and Bill for a family celebration at the boarding house. They stuffed themselves on meat loaf, potatoes, green beans, chocolate cake, and canned peaches. Charles lingered way past the "old folks" bedtimes, but no one took issue with it. Alice drove him home around midnight, when he took out his pens and began.

> *October 24, 1942*
> *My Darling Alice:*
>
> *I am writing you this letter because I hope to express my thoughts to you on this day. I want so much to tell you all the things that are in my heart on this, the greatest day in my life. Your accepting my ring has given me happiness beyond expression. Your loving me has made me so very humble. The joy of that love is endless.*
>
> *You said tonight that no matter what happened, you would always love me. My dear, it will be that great love of ours that will carry us on beyond the darkness which seems to be descending upon us, and carry us into the light of our life together. There will come a day before too long when we can be married and begin a new life. I pray to God it will be soon. Without hope, life is not worth living and*

so we must keep our hope for a bright future. I am sure it will come. Our love will carry us there.

There are some things that cannot be expressed even in writing. The love I bear for you is one of those things. I shall never be able to tell you how dear you are to me. The ring I am giving you is but an outward sign of my love for you. The inward love, no one shall ever know. I love you with all the love a man can bear for a woman. My darling, you alone shall share my life.

We have known each other for four years now. That time has passed quickly. Yet, I feel I have known you forever. In that time we have learned a great deal about each other. I suppose we really know very little. Out of our companionship has come our love and it is good. I feel sure that if God had not meant it this way, we would have parted long ago. Now, my darling, we shall never really be separated no matter how far apart we may be on this earth; we shall always be together in our love.

So my dear, we must have faith in each other and in our future. With that faith we shall conquer all that may come before us. Our love will live forever.

With deepest love,
Marvin

Chapter 13

Gathered Here

My father used his middle name, Marvin, in correspondence up until the day he married Alice. After that no one called him Marvin except his mother Clara. In the early years with Alice, he was Charles. By the mid-sixties, everyone called him Mac, "except for Bob who called me George because I already had too many names to keep track of," he laughed. His own name-switching tickled him, even after he became the director of student records at OSU, where he spent all day dealing with thousands of students' names, sorting them out, correctly spelling them, and changing them. He groused about people who hyphenated their names because they didn't fit into the allowable spaces on forms. He refused to give Marsha and me middle names, telling Mother, "They'll end up with one more name through marriage."

As it turned out, Marsha picked up three last names along the way and then reverted to McClintock. I kept McClintock all along.

At the time of their marriage, he was eager to give Alice his McClintock name. He wanted the straight life, despite his likely experiences with gay men in New York—or maybe because of them.

86

WEDDING DAY

He grew more insistent that they marry soon. Life in New York tugged at him and became an escape hatch over and over again in the future, because he didn't want to give up his identity as a good son and a fine husband for Alice. Other men had the fortitude to bear the stigma of being labeled a "pervert," a "fornicator," or "sexual deviant," but the closet would be his only choice. He wanted Clara's doting, Bata's pies, and a Norman Rockwell family. His loyalty to folks back home was stronger than his loyalty to himself.

He wrote her a letter on March 15, 1943, in a melancholy mood.

After reading your letter, I just wanted to take the next train home and marry you right then and there. It does seem that we are letting precious time slip by while we cannot be married. We could have such a perfect setup if you could get a job here in the city. We could have our own apartment. Maybe now we're living too much for the future and ignoring the present just as before we ignored the inevitable future and lived only in the present. I know furlough marriages are not wise. But who does the wise thing these days? Maybe it's high time we stopped being so practical and did something a little foolish for a change. As your mother says, we'd be a lot happier if we weren't so serious-minded. "Nothing ventured, nothing gained."

My very dear, I know our love shall last forever. It can carry us through the war unsullied. But why deny ourselves happiness? Don't we owe it to ourselves to snatch a little of it here and there? Oh, tell me, tell me darling, if I am wrong? I know I'm torturing myself with all this and probably tearing your heart out, too. But I love you so madly I want you for my very own wife more than anything else in the world. Oh darling—with all my love, Marvin.

The wedding was hastily planned for early October, a year after the engagement, to coincide with a furlough Charles arranged from his post in New York City. They had just six weeks to plan and pull off the wedding, so Bata called Reverend Doctor Reed, who scheduled an evening service at Indianola Presbyterian Church. Donald's commanding officer granted him leave to play the part of best man. Donald would wear his officer rank dress blues, and Charles would wear his brass-buttoned uniform. Alice and Bata picked out simple bridesmaid dresses for Mom's best friend and her sister-in-law, arranged for a florist and a photographer. Grandma Bata searched through her recipe file to find the butter cream layer cake she felt honored to make.

Alice found the dress she wanted in a small downtown shop. Thirty years later, I stood in the parlor of a Presbyterian church as she had, repeating history, and wearing that dress. Since she was generously shaped, the creamy satin bodice, full skirt, and train that flowed to the floor provided the alteration lady extra yards of fabric to work with in revamping it for me. In her pictures, Mom is posed in the half circle of a long satin train, showing off the classy row of eighteen pearl buttons down each sleeve and wearing a veil with a beaded crown.

At my 1970s unconventional wedding, the dress had been altered; it was smaller and simpler to fit the trendy hippie-girl culture. When Mom offered me my grandmother Clara's diamond ring (since she had died and we never bury rings), I turned it down in favor of matching gold bands a jeweler designed from a piece of coral my fiancé and I found at the ocean. Pretentious things were suspect in the seventies. But in 1944, in the midst of the Second World War, Alice and Charles had high hopes for their future and an elegant formal wedding.

Mom and I had more than a dress in common. We both felt uncertain, but what bride doesn't? She was the more stoic. In the midst of my ceremony I began to cry. My father slid his hand into his back pocket and passed his handkerchief to me. He understood unpredictable futures. After I dabbed my nose and eyes, my husband put it in his pocket as a keepsake for me.

Was Alice feeling more confident in her choice of men, having declared love and trust in every letter to Charles for more than a year? She selected him as much through her mother's discernment as her own, and this respect would have to hold her in the marriage through repeated insults. It occurs to me that on my wedding day I was just as young and equally naïve. I like to think I'm more evolved than my mother, with the courage to end a bad marriage, but in truth I didn't end my marriage, my husband did. He chose to get out of harm's way as I raged. There are no get-out-of-jail-free cards handed to you on the day you marry. We both stood before a minister—mother listened politely to her scholarly preacher, Dr. Reed, and I listened to an obscure Biblical sermon on fidelity from the book of Hosea preached by a seminary colleague in a belted brown monk robe with an overgrown beard and shoulder-length hair, looking like a church parlor picture of Jesus. A soloist sang the Lord's Prayer at mother's wedding. My husband played his guitar and we sang a duet at ours—a song from the musical *Pippin* describing love as more than a touch or feeling and likely to send us reeling.

1974

Home from college on a break, I stopped by Grandma's house to have a front-window chat.

"Your mom had the jitters, which is understandable, and I gave her a little pep talk at the house before the ceremony." Grandma offered me her version of my parents' wedding. "Your father has been a good man for her, and he was head-over-heels in love with your mother." She paused, and I thought she might cry. "It was hard to see her move out," she said, wandering around back in time and a little lost amidst the floral wallpaper in Alice's room, recalling a picture of Charles in his uniform next to Alice's bed.

"Go on, Grandma," I said to call her back.

"In the dressing room at the church, your mom pulled on her stockings and a blue garter that Clara had worn at her own wedding and spruced up with new satin ribbons. It covered the whole gamut—something old, something new, something borrowed, and blue, all in one fell swoop. And then she put on that gorgeous dress with the train so long it nearly pulled her over backward. I was so proud of her. She was all smiles when Sam walked her down the aisle."

I'd heard about Grandpa Sam's big guffaw.

"The lights were dimmed, and the ushers lit the candles, which were secured with ribbons to the end of each pew. The organist played Wagner's *Bridal March,* and we all stood up to watch them come in.

"I heard Sam say, 'I love you sweetie.'

"Alice leaned closer to him and whispered, 'I love you too, Daddy.'

"When they got to the front, he placed Alice's hand in your father's hand, and Rev. Dr. Reed began. 'Dearly beloved, we are gathered here today in the sight of God to unite this man and this woman,' etc. you know how it goes.

"And then he asked, 'Who gives this woman to be married to this man?'

"You know Sam; he stepped forward like a soldier under orders. 'Her mother and I do.' He said, and then he stepped back."

I knew what was coming next, so I added, "He laid his hand directly on top of a burning candle, muttering those now infamous words, 'Damn, who put that there?'"

"He was hopping up and down, blowing on his fingers."

Grandma's eyes danced like candle flames, and her smile took over her whole face. Then she continued. "Everyone heard him. They were silent for a minute, knowing they shouldn't laugh, but finally they couldn't stop themselves. Your father's shoulders shook, and Alice blushed. The minister paused until Sam sat down. With order restored, they said the usual 'I dos' and 'I wills' in their proper places. Charles flipped back Alice's veil, lifted her chin, and sweetly kissed her."

EARLY YEARS

KAREN AND MARSHA IN THE BACKYARD

Chapter 14

Groundbreaking

1953

I was raised in a time of hope and procreation. Mother and Father, like thousands of post-war soldiers and their wives, were determined to make the American dream come true. My father left behind the option that many post-war gay soldiers took—of coming out and remaining in New York City, giving birth to the gay liberation movement.

The dream of "settling down" with a wife and kids wasn't shared by Walther P. Michael. He became a U.S. citizen during the war, and served in the continental U.S., Hawaii, New Guinea, and the Philippines until 1945 when he returned to New York City and enrolled in graduate studies at Columbia University. While immersing himself in reading and writing about world economics, Walther's life in New York provided him ample room to develop his identity. Could Father have met Walther in New York during the months they were both stationed there? Would Walther have followed him to Columbus? I have to be content with not knowing.

The day Father came home from work with a deed of sale for a quarter-acre parcel on Ridgecliff Road, he swept Mom into his arms and kissed her confidently. From their cramped campus apartment, he could already picture a red brick, two-bedroom, one-bath house in the new neighborhood that was still a cornfield. The land, to the northwest of Columbus and an easy drive to the university, had sustained a farmer's family back four generations. But the postwar boom had expanded the city limits, and people with means were destined to create suburbs. These were Betty Crocker days, and families were acculturated by images of curl-coiffed Caucasian women in flouncy skirts with white ruffled aprons who provided their families with satisfying food cooked on miraculously efficient new appliances.

At four years old, my sister Marsha was an easy child to raise— playful and curious. She had blue eyes, a slightly stubby nose, and gorgeous light brown curly hair all the way down to her shoulders. Alice was pregnant again with me on the way when my parents bought normalcy with prosperity.

Father held the deed high overhead, and they danced a little two-step and finished with a Fred and Ginger twirl. She said the street name out loud to be sure of it. "Ridgecliff Road," she said, thinking it an odd name for an old cornfield. I notice that in the West, where I now live, we name our streets by their characteristics. For example, streets with view names actually have views. Oak Street is lined with oak trees. Midwest towns in the forties were built in an aspirational era. Ohio flatlander real estate developers broke with all conventional wisdom and, despite having never even driven south to the Appalachian Mountains, chose street names with vistas and valleys, ridges and canyons. Perhaps the developer had just gotten a postcard from a cousin who lived in the Rockies. Ridgecliff Road was a mile long and entirely flat; no matter, that's what they named it.

Father's newly purchased plot, on the north edge of the original farm, had several large ash trees on it, part of a former windbreak, and though the plan had been to level all the trees, Father insisted that the developer move the house slightly back from the road to keep several of them in the front yard. As we kids grew, these trees became the center of our universe. They were maypoles in the spring and our neighborhood "Olly olly oxen free" zone in the summer. We couldn't climb them, because their smooth trunks and enormous limbs branched out way above our heads. Even Rita Jean, our tall and athletic neighbor, who regularly made outside shots at the basketball hoop attached to her garage, could just barely touch the bottom of the lowest branch on her highest lay-up jump. We squeezed between the tree trunks—invisibly spying on kids in the neighborhood as they came home from the elementary school up Kirkham Road. Even peering through binoculars from our front porch, we couldn't quite see the school. But to this day, I am sure that if I could have climbed to the top of those trees, I could have picked out Miss Tubbs' Quonset hut, where I spent my kindergarten year.

Those trees became the signposts by which we found our way home from school, or to the church down on the corner where we'd soon be baptized, and the way we told friends where we lived. Our trees were famous and saved us from having to remember street numbers. We'd just point to those glorious trees, standing tall and feeling proud to own them, since the developers had clear-cut the other properties and replanted them with spindly trees and ugly shrubs. Under the shade of those massive trees, we set up a card table with Mother's white tablecloth with red geranium patterned edges and stacked up little paper cups in which to serve lemonade in their shade. We sold enough to buy new roller skates.

The ceremonial groundbreaking for our house had taken place on a cold morning in late April 1953, eight months before my birth. In our family, we did rituals right. We were a clan of Presbyterians on one side and Methodists on the other. My grandparents Chet and Clara believed in a non-sectarian God and thus attended whichever congregation was close enough for a reasonable walk in all seasons. Grandma Bata, the family philosopher, was staunchly Presbyterian. No one knew what Grandpa Sam believed in, but he got up every Sunday morning, shaved, put on his best suit, and went with Bata to church. He went without grousing beforehand or commenting afterward. My mother's acquaintance with God had been inevitable, since she'd grown up across the street from the church. We took Grandma literally when she called her church, "God's house." Most of our family rituals took place in that house, including several confirmations and three generations of weddings.

My parents became charter members in the newly forming Presbyterian congregation that was also breaking ground down the block from our spot on Ridgecliff Road. Before the foundation was poured, Mom planned on this new church becoming our second home.

I'm looking at a blurry black-and-white snapshot during an overcast day on that muddy field that would become our home. Grandpa Chet stands proudly in the foreground wearing his heavy winter coat and gray felt hat, one foot securely on the shovel ready to cut through frozen ground. The shovel was decorated with a huge ribbon Mother had likely kept from Christmas. In the picture, my father is beaming with so much pride that the Polaroid can't fully capture it. I'm surprised that there isn't a Presbyterian minister at the family groundbreaking ceremony, unless he stepped aside during the photo. This is a holy ritual, nevertheless, and the congregation has gathered. The grandmothers are in their finely tailored warm woolen coats, leather gloves, and Sunday hats. Marsha, standing waist high to Mother, leans into her long overcoat to keep warm. Mom is not yet showing, but nausea, combined with the torture of insatiable hunger, has increased the dark circles beneath her eyes. As the shovel cuts through the partially frozen ground, she feels secure about everything; she and Father have now sealed their promises to one another with a major investment. She picks up Marsha, who leans her head against the warm fur collar of Mom's coat. "That's it," says Chet. "Let's head on over to the house for coffee and bridge." They might as well have said, "Amen!"

In the following weeks, Father went to the building site every evening after work and stared into what he called "the mud hole" while the contractors dug the foundation. *I don't deserve all of this,* he'd think, *and yet I am so thankful for it.*

He had obtained a job at the VA hospital working on a ward with shell-shocked soldiers. He was emotionally drawn into the misery of combat exhaustion, butchered limbs, faces burned beyond recognition, and the constant smell of infection and cleansers. To calm what they referred to as the "terror of neurosis," soldiers were given sedatives, and due to a lack of psychiatrists to treat them, people newly trained, like Father, were sent in to interview them about their war experiences to relieve their stress and encourage them to talk about their battlefield experiences. "I can do so little to help them," he told Mom. "And what can I say to them, having never gone into combat myself?" He became nervous and lost sleep—emotionally drained by their trauma.

I was on a visit home to see Mother in the late '70s. We sat next to each other on the lime green couch, as we had for years while I still lived at home. She described the year Father worked with shell-shocked veterans as "a very dark time" in his life. It grew harder and harder for him to mug before the camera and to play the part of a proud expectant father. He kept a personal journal of his work with shattered soldiers at a veteran's hospital. My mother showed it to me after his death, but as I reached across for a closer look, she pulled her hand back and tucked it under her thigh between the seat cushions. She did not allow Marsha or me to read it, and while she kept his other journals, she destroyed this one as part of her lifelong pattern to protect "her girls" from our father's pain. Within a year he found a new job at Ohio State University, working with veterans returning to school on the GI Bill.

While the house was built and the exterior looked good, their marriage hit its first rough period. She puffed on her cigarette and told me matter-of-factly, "Honey, you were our last sex." In the cartoon bubble over my head I asked, "Now what am I supposed to say?" I was shocked to learn that my mother had been celibate many more years than not, but I said nothing. I had learned by then that I had to wait for the stories, since questions were viewed as inquisitions. The more I overtly asked for the truth, the more shame sucked her down into silence.

At first she made it seem like his depression was the reason their sexual connection ended. "He just withdrew from everything and everyone," she said. "He was overwhelmed by the suffering those men were going through—our sex life had been clumsy and unsatisfying for both of us, so eventually we just gave it up." She misinterpreted my rising anxiety. "But don't think you weren't wanted, sweetie," she said, unfolding her legs and curling them back up under her on the opposite side. "We intentionally had intercourse in order to conceive you." In this moment, was I supposed to thank her?

Her words slapped me the way Grandma Bata had one night in a big storm. I had been shaking so badly she was afraid I'd hurt myself, so my normally controlled and gentle Grandma Bata gave me a sharp slap across the face and said, "Calm down." I felt like that again throughout this conversation. I'm not sure what was going on when she told me this, but it was consistent with her emotional over-sharing and her detail under-sharing. I instinctively sat up and relocated myself a little farther down the couch. Kids shouldn't know these things about parents, don't want to know "yucky stuff" about their parents' sex lives, don't usually need to know—unless shame has such a noxious, lingering effect that healing requires new information. In my case, intentionally concealed information protected them against guilt and shame.

Their little brick house came together quickly, and by September, Mom's third trimester fatigue was alleviated by hopeful anticipation. Contractors had hoisted up the wooden frame, bricklayers were building the fireplace, and roofers sheathed and shingled until sundown. My father was there every day after work, loosening his tie and admiring his paradise. The satisfaction of seeing his dream turn into a home moved him to tears on more than one occasion. The house became strong, and his life needed something this solid. Or perhaps his tears fell freely in the dark, as he stood out there alone, knowing that as the walls were hammered together, his marriage was already coming apart.

On weekends, he brought Mom over to the house for a walk-through. When not at the site, he spent hours laying out his flower garden on graph paper with circles for trees and bushes, shapes a bird could recognize in a flyover. She'd find him late at night, poring over garden books she'd brought him from the library. He viewed his backyard like a painter drawing on a canvas. He also laid out the interior of the house, except for the kitchen, which he left to Mom. He drew the rooms to scale and then cut out little couches, desks, beds, and chairs to try out in different configurations.

You may now be saying, dear reader, we should have known my father was gay because he loved art, interior design, and gardening, culturally stereotypical of gay men. When the house painters arrived, he had color chips in hand. When the furniture truck brought over our family's meager apartment remnants, he directed the crew. He recovered from his secondary trauma by designing a peaceful place. They moved to Ridgecliff Road a month before I was born.

"You come back here with that wooden spoon, Marsha!" Mom sounded mad but wasn't. Tired and bulging at eight months pregnant, she had to walk around boxes to find my sister, who giggled at their game of hide-and-seek. When Mom bent over to retrieve the stolen spoon, she rubbed her back and hoisted herself up again. "This is a big baby," she mumbled to no one in particular. "Here, honey," she said, pulling plastic jugs from a box, "you can play with these. See if you can find the lids that match." The back door slammed, and Mac tapped the mud off his sandals.

"I'm never going to tame this land," he said to her, kissing her cheek and walking to the living room, scooping up my sister to relocate her and hug her as he went. "I've got the bulbs in, at least," he said in the direction of the kitchen.

He had, in fact, tamed the field, as she knew he would. Over the summer he had dumped compost and manure in flower beds on the edges of the property, creating an elaborate curvaceous frame for the sod that would fill in the center. He spent more than a few minutes the following summer yelling out the back door at Marsha to "Stay off that lawn!" Alongside the garage, he built trellises and planted purple clematis, climbing Irish ivy, and Clotted Cream Jasmine. By the time of my November birth, the boxes were all unpacked. A full row of brick and stucco houses was completed along the street's south side. Their inhabitants, no longer sacrificing for the war effort, were ready for a life of peace.

SAM AND BATA LIVINGSTON

Chapter 15

Thanksgiving

Grandma Bata could not be expected to tell a story without elaboration. She taught me to be the preacher that I later became. Thinking how lonely she surely was living all by herself after Grandpa Sam died, I made a point to frequently visit her little "house"—a first floor retirement apartment near the library where Mom worked. Driving up in front of her place, I could see her looking out the window for me. She'd made pie, of course, and I could smell cherries as she welcomed me in. On either side of the lace-curtained window in "the front room" as she called it, were two armchairs, set up for prayer and chatting. Between the chairs, a spindle-legged two-drawer table with glass knobs sat covered in a crocheted doily she had purchased at a church bazaar. She kept her black-bound King James Bible at easy reach, along with a little book called *A Gift from the Sea,* by Anne Morrow Lindbergh. In the drawers she kept bulletins and sermon copies by Rev. Swinburne at the church, which she regularly mailed to me.

Despite years of knowing the truth about my parents' "marital problem," Grandma Bata overlooked the facts like she peered over the tops of her reading glasses when talking to us. She insisted repeatedly they were deeply in love with each other. I could call her a co-conspirator, but that sounds too harsh. We all compensated. She was in her late seventies at the time of my visit, an age when happy memories grow stronger and sad ones fade away. By describing my birthday to me, she could show me the true love my parents had for each other and how delighted all of them had been that I came along.

As Bata told it, Alice was moving slowly that morning, lugging around thirty-five extra pounds. She was not basking in the glow of pregnancy when Bata called her.

"I'm *so* ready to be done with this one." It was Thanksgiving Day, 1953, and while Alice usually loved family gatherings at holidays, on that day she was exhausted.

"Mother, I look like a hippo! Even the loosest things I own are tight now. I got dressed, but my blouse won't button all the way, and I hate looking in the mirror."

"Not long to go, my dear. Put the receiver on your belly a minute."

"What?"

"I want to talk to the baby." Alice decided to play along and could faintly hear Bata talking.

"Come on now; give your mother a break. We're ready for you."

"Okay, Mom, I think the baby heard you and gave me a swift kick! And don't count on me to eat anything today. There's no room in my stomach. I'm afraid I won't be much help today either."

"With Clara and me both cooking, there's nothing to worry about. You can sit all day in Pop's lounge chair. Chet will keep Marsha happy playing Crazy Eights."

Alice noticed Marsha bundled in her navy blue coat, carting around her favorite stuffed bear.

"I gotta go now, Mom. Everyone is ready, and I'll see you soon."

The first cold snow of the season was still piled along the street, melting in the sunshine. Charles had carefully backed the car out of the driveway and loaded in Alice and Marsha. He brought along the dinner rolls and the hospital bag just in case. Alice felt the baby becoming more active, though it was a week ahead of her due date. The doctor said that second children often come early, then laughed and said, "Don't worry, Alice, babies don't just fall out."

They had a short drive over to Chet and Clara's house on Mount-view Road, two doors down from Bata and Sam.

"Weren't we lucky to find a house near to your Grandma Clara and Grandpa Chet?" Grandma asked me.

"I loved running back and forth between your houses, always finding someone to hang out with—a grandma in the kitchen or a grandpa in a garden hammock."

"When your parents married, we never imagined we would become so close, playing bridge two or three nights a week and sharing holidays. We had such great times together." She was lost in nostalgia.

"What happened on my birthday?" I prompted.

"Oh yes. Sam and I put on our boots and walked down to Chet and Clara's with my three holiday pies."

"Mincemeat, pumpkin, and pecan." It was always the same three pies.

When everyone else arrived, Grandma Bata was in the kitchen with Clara making gravy. Marsha came through the house in a flash and scooted past Grandpa Chet in order to duck under Grandma Bata's ruffled apron for a hug.

"You're looking ready to burst, little lady," Chet told Alice, opening the door widely. The familiar smells of roasting turkey caused Alice to breathe it all in as her mother reached across her belly and gave her a hug and kiss. She offered to help.

"No, no, just set a spell. We've got it covered."

"Set a spell" was Grandma's way of saying "Take a load off." The word was "sit," of course, but she'd lived her early adulthood on the Ohio River near Kentucky. When you are from Southern Ohio, which is pronounced *O-high-ah*, "sit" comes out "set." Mom would have been happy to "set a spell" that day and headed for Chet's lounge chair.

Marsha was soon on Grandpa Sam's lap, watching him play games with his face. He pulled on his left earlobe and his protruding tongue moved to the left side of his mouth. She giggled and pulled on his right earlobe, which caused his tongue to pull over to the right side. She squealed, and they repeated the game a few times. "Please, Grandpa, touch your nose!" Sam had a very long nose and a talent for touching his tongue to it, which was so gross it was funny. Grandma liked recalling how happy it made Sam to play this game with us kids, even if it made her miss him. He was gone by my tenth birthday. Grandma momentarily swallowed back some tears. I wondered what it felt like to lose someone you love.

"Mac was always a gentleman with Alice; he was very attentive that day," she said.

"Pop's got ginger ale, root beer, or how 'bout a little of his nightly claret? Maybe that would encourage the little bugger to fall asleep or make a descent, right? What'll it be, little lady?" he asked her, with a Groucho Marx accent, waving an imaginary cigar.

"The Vernors on ice and not a lot—thanks, sweetie." She felt queasy.

Grandma saw Alice reposition herself in Chet's chair and flinch. The first really big contraction is unmistakable. She stood up slowly and went into the bathroom and shut the door. She had barely stepped across the linoleum when she felt an uncontrollable stream of water gush down her legs. She lunged for the toilet and grabbed a towel bar, which crashed to the floor as she sat down.

"Is everything okay in there?" Grandma was instantly at the door.

"Mother, could you come in here, please?"

"I'm right here."

"Be careful, Mom—I think the floor is wet." Bata saw the crashed towel bar.

"Well, well, the towel is handier now." She began mopping up. Then she hollered out the door to the others, "Everything's all right, nothing to worry about."

Grandma had given birth to two babies over ten pounds each, so she was pretty calm.

Well, this one may be coming a little quickly, she thought. "Let me go tell Charles."

Charles brought the car around, then went back to check on Alice. Grandpa Chet grabbed her coat and met them at the front door. Grandma Clara scooped Marsha up in her arms.

"We get to have Thanksgiving dinner with you all to ourselves," she told Marsha, who was squirming around. "Mommy's going to the hospital to have the baby, and when she's done, we'll all go see them both!"

"Can we take Momma some dinner and pie?" Marsha asked.

They sarcastically chided me every Thanksgiving meal thereafter for having disrupted my mother's meal.

"Sure, honey, but your momma won't feel much like eating."

With my grandmothers standing arm in arm and Marsha tucked between them, Charles loaded Alice into the sedan and took off. A little over an hour later, he called them. At a healthy eight pounds and seven ounces, I'd been checked out by the doctors and returned to a bassinet at my mother's side.

"We were so happy you came into this world, sweetie," Grandma said, patting my arm across the table.

Grandma-style, I like making up a variation to the ending of this story. After my father hung up the phone in the fathers' waiting room, he asked the nurse to escort him down the hall to see me. Quietly opening the door, he tiptoed into the room to find Mom and me resting, and he stared dumbstruck into the bassinet. He leaned over and kissed Mom lightly on the forehead. When she didn't stir, he sat down and took her hand without a word, a little lost in wonder and gratitude. He fell in love with me at that very moment. And if I ever doubted it, Grandmother was there to reassure me.

"We all loved you very much—your father, too," Grandma said, providing a simple and satisfying ending to her story.

Chapter 16

Mom's Little Ditties

Mom sang what she called "little ditties" in our red brick house. Sitting at the dining table snapping the ends off peas, she entertained herself, and when caught in the act, laughed at herself, noting that "the simple are easily amused." At bedtime, after teeth brushing, putting on jammies and a few minutes on my knees for prayer while she stood in the doorway, she sat on the edge of the bed next to me.

Her alto voice soothed me like honey dripped over cornbread. She sang "Mairzy Doats," a nonsense song about animals, including a baby lamb—a "kid" that ate ivy.

"Would you eat ivy?" She feigned disapproval.

I nodded *yes*. She played along.

"We've got some ivy in the backyard. I'll cook some up for breakfast."

She tucked the blankets under my chin, and I begged for one more, knowing she always closed out the night with the song "Skidamarink a-dink, a-dink, Skidamarink a-doo."

She loved me all day long, the song said.

She turned off the light so all we could see was the hallway nightlight's faint glow.

Almost whispering, she finished the little ditty.

"I love you!"

I snuggled in and hummed myself to sleep.

Mom's ability to memorize lyrics could have landed her on *Name that Tune,* which we watched on the black-and-white television that joined our family when I was six. As kids we threw out a line to see what she'd do with it and almost never stumped her. Always on pitch, with a decent range, and a gravelly vibrato, Mom filled our lives with music. Gathering up laundry, she drummed a beat on the hamper: "Down in the meadow in an itty-bitty pool, swam three little fishies and a momma fishie too. 'Swim,' said the mama fishy, 'swim if you can,' and they swam and they swam right over the dam." Even with a great singing voice, she still didn't want to be a soloist. "Join in now" she said, and we were happy to oblige. "Boop boop dittem dattem what-tem chu!"

This habit of singing made her appear to be always in a good mood. Having a house to call her own in a new suburb, with two healthy children, she thought it couldn't get any better than that—and so it looked. The lyrics were nonsensical, and who cared—her marriage was nonsensical too. Might as well do a little song and dance.

Mom was home after school every day without fail, feeling proud of her commitment to us. She worked at the library from nine to one and came home to cooking, washing dishes, and checking our homework. One day she was imagining herself to be in an act, like the Andrews Sisters singing an old Al Jolson tune. "Toot, toot, Tootsie, goodbye," she sang, dish rag spinning around as she danced. She swayed from side to side, shoulders leading, totally absorbed in her music. "Toot, toot, Tootsie, goodbye, toot, toot, Tootsie, don't cry. That choo choo train that takes me away from you, no words can tell how sad it makes me. . . ."

When I thought she was distracted, I crossed through the kitchen toward the back door, heading to the yard to get my bike and find some mischief.

"Hey, where ya going?" she asked, stopping me.

"Caught me," I said with an impish grin.

"Come on now," she hollered, "sing it with me." She flicked a towel out from the waistband of her apron and spun around pigeon-toed, swiveling her hips, with her left hand pointed to the ceiling waving with the rhythms in her head. She moved to block my exit, "Watch for the mail, I'll never fail, if you don't get a letter then you'll know I'm in jail." She threw the towel in my direction and started into the chorus again. "Pull back on it, sweetie," she said, and I did. "Now smash your toes into the floor like squishing bugs," she said, singing another line. I got to giggling and raised both hands. Dropping the towel, I was off balance and fell back against the refrigerator, slid down and onto the floor—still laughing. She scooped me up and twirled me in both arms, holding my shoulders. Steadying me, she pointed me toward the door, swatted my backside lightly. "Now be good and have fun," she said, which when I was older seemed like an oxymoron.

I skipped down the back steps that day thinking about my beautiful, talented mother. She deserved a larger stage than the eight feet square of linoleum in our kitchen. I planned to use my magic wand, say "bibbidi-bobbidi-boo," and put her in a spotlight on stage with the Andrews Sisters or maybe conjure up Fred Astaire to spin around the stage with her.

In our theatrical family, a large open space in the basement of the Ridgecliff Road house was given to Marsha and me as a performance space. Boxes of discarded clothes and shoes became costumes. Dad went over and claimed a twelve-by-fifteen foot square of old rug at his parents' house when they installed new tufted wall-to-wall carpet. He stuffed the remnant into the trunk of his car, put a red flag on the end of it, and drove it slowly across town.

"What are you doing with that old ratty thing?" Mom had that disapproving tone.

"It's for the girls to play on rather than the bare concrete." He hauled it down the stairs.

He strung a curtain of sheets across the room on a sturdy wire and mounted floodlights on our "stage." He built low shelves around the perimeter of the room for our toy boxes and roller skates, and when he placed his Lincoln Log set down there, he told us we could use it only under his strict supervision. We kept to this prohibition even when our parents were out of sight, as Dad knew we would. We were obedient girls, as if we intuited that there was a fragile cord of love around our family which would fray or break if conflicts arose. To keep everything copasetic, we all lived happily in our fantasy worlds of play-acting. We stayed in character.

We memorized Disney movies—all we needed was an apple and a few stuffed animals for dwarves. Marsha got a record player for her twelfth birthday, and Mom brought home a discarded LP of *Cinderella* for us. The groove of "Someday My Prince Will Come" became so worn down that it skipped.

Some days the basement was a dance studio. Marsha assumed the role of a strict Russian dance teacher since she took ballet, tap, and jazz lessons every week at the place we called "Jeanie Borsky's School of Ballet Torture." My parents sent her there to help with what they quietly referred to as her "weight problem," but I was a skinny kid sister. She had tap shoes and cool costumes, along with my envy. Grab a few extra cookies after school, and you get rewarded with dance classes. Maybe she was bullied about her size at school, but people didn't talk about bullying back then. I'm just looking for a reason to excuse her behavior, because she clearly enjoyed taunting me. At ballet time, she pulled out an old wooden cane we had in the costume box, hauled over one of Dad's sawhorses to use as a ballet barre, and stood me alongside of it, then whapped the inside of my knee with the cane.

"Turn that knee out," she barked. "Mrs. Borsky will hit you even harder if you don't turn out that knee."

Marsha licked her lips like a cat that has cornered a mouse. After a few more whacks, I hissed at her, went to the puppet box, and began a script for the play I was writing about a prince and princess. She whined and eventually helped me perform my play. I hollered upstairs for Mom to come watch it, which she always did.

"Bravo!" She smiled, clapping wildly, "bravo!" She was on her feet after the puppet show.

"You girls are the best." We took our bows. "Magnificent!" she said, and went on and on until she excused herself to check on dinner.

We had everything we needed in our performance space. On my eighth birthday, Mom brought a projector home from the library and a couple of movies—a short Mickey Mouse cartoon and an art film called *The Red Balloon* by French filmmaker Albert La Morisse that had been out since 1956.

"This is such a great movie," she said. "You'll love it, it's all about a red balloon, and that can be your birthday theme. I'll get some red balloons to decorate with and make you a red devil's food cake. How would that be?" I had nothing to go on except her enthusiasm.

"Invite your friends," she said, and we put together a list of half a dozen kids. The neighbor girl and her obnoxious brother came along at the last minute at my sister's insistence. Since I was born on Thanksgiving, Mom felt badly that I was always forced to celebrate my birthday with all the grandparents and eat turkey, so she tried to make my birthdays extra special by having parties a week ahead of time. She thought that the red balloon party was going to be really grand, over the top.

"It's an award-winning feature film," she said, sounding like the announcer on the Ed Sullivan show. "Here's a reeaally big movie!"

My sister looked over at me and rolled her eyes.

On the day of the party, Mom put popcorn in little paper sacks and tied the red balloons on the front porch and the handrails leading to our basement movie theater. The lights went dark and we laughed a lot watching the Mickey Mouse short cartoon.

"Sit still now while I change the reel." She put the huge film spool with *The Red Balloon* onto the projector. It was a movie about a boy and his overly large round, red balloon walking around a dismally gray Paris neighborhood. At about ten minutes in, Robbie was smacking Peter on the back, and the girls had snuck over to the toy box and grabbed a doll from her cradle. Popcorn began spilling out of bags, and some of it was tossed around just short of a school food fight. The movie ran on, and the little boy's balloon was chased and shot down from the sky by a gang of hostile children. By then, I hoped none of my friends were watching and glanced at Mom. *What was she thinking?* I saw tears flooding her eyes and sneaking down her cheeks. My embarrassing mom was either crying over the death of a red balloon or sad about something she couldn't talk about. In my loud theater voice, I told the other kids (though I was going on hope) "It's almost done" when I saw the movie take a brighter turn. Balloons from all over Paris came to the boy, who grabbed onto their strings and floated off into the air at the end. When it was over, the kids stood up and clapped, not so much for the film, but because it was over. We happily climbed the stairs and gathered at the dining room table to eat the—sure enough, she'd pulled it off—red balloon-shaped birthday cake.

Chapter 17

Independence Days

FOURTH OF JULY 1958

My beanstalk father hoisted me up on his shoulders, and we strained our necks looking down the street. For three miles down Tremont Avenue, the sidewalks bustled with kids and their parents wearing red, white, and blue and waving little American flags. Little kids spilled out of their folding chairs into the street. Older kids rode the route to show off their crepe paper and glittered bicycles. We were all looking for the clown truck, a huge semi with open double doors in the back. All along the route, a dozen clowns emerged with fistfuls of helium balloons to distribute—one to every kid on the route. I started bouncing eagerly when we saw the distant truck, and Dad grabbed my ankle more tightly.

"Whoa there, par-dner," he said, Texas-style. "Settle down or you'll buck off this horse." Marsha laughed and began hopping up and down. I grabbed his forehead and leaned over his head until I saw them.

"They're coming!" I shouted. Balloons galore.

After the clowns passed by, everyone on the whole street settled down. In the distance, we could see three guys coming toward us. They were young, barely in their teens, wearing soiled and torn Rev-

114

olutionary War uniforms. The guy on the left had a bandage around his head, caked brown with dirt and blood. He played a steady solemn beat on a leather drum. The middle soldier waved a flag with thirteen stars in a circle, frayed and pockmarked by bullet holes. The one on the right played "When Johnny Comes Marching Home Again" on his tarnished piccolo. My father wiped his eyes with one sleeve and began crying in earnest. He hoisted me over his head and handed me to Mother so he could pull out his handkerchief. Every year the parade started in this way, and every year he cried.

The only year we missed the clowns and the soldiers was the very next year when my mother and her friends decided it would be great fun to have a neighborhood float in the parade. She contacted a guy with a huge flatbed truck, which he parked on the street, and then she phoned everyone on the block to come decorate it. Our float theme that year was based on the hit single "I Told the Witch Doctor." All the kids in the neighborhood dressed up in imaginary witch doctor costumes—grass skirts, paper headdresses, and green face paint. I wore a simple one-piece bathing suit and rode the whole route in a large cast-iron kettle set atop a fake open wood fire pit. I hated the whole gig. I could barely see over the pot's edge, and I had to stand up the entire route. My sister and Rita Jean stood over me with drawn weapons—they had large paddles with which to stir the pot and prod me to keep standing up and waving. My parents walked alongside us—to keep them from killing me, no doubt—though they didn't pay much attention. They were chatting, laughing, and smiling at neighbors, oblivious to my suffering. I'd been denied my prime spot on my adored father's shoulders and never got a balloon. It was such a bad experience that, even when Marsha and Rita Jean grew older and I could have joined them in the decorated bike section, I chose to sit it out on the sidelines with Mother and Father instead.

I have always kept my love for small town parades and sit along our Main Street on the Fourth of July every year. Since the witch doctor fiasco, I have avoided being in them. But when I was forty-three years old, I said, "Yes, I'd be honored," when I was invited to walk with the local chapter of Parents and Friends of Lesbians and Gays. I carried a hand-painted sign upon which I'd written "I love my gay father." A passing truck honked, and the guy on the passenger side yelled, "Too bad he's going to hell!" But a young woman on the parade route stopped me. "Could you take a picture of me with your sign?" she asked. "I want to send it to my father." That year I was the one crying.

My parents "held their own," as the saying goes, while they raised Marsha and me. Mother went to lunch with her friend Frances twice a week and chatted with her by phone. Frances leaned toward me at Mother's funeral and said, "You have no idea what your mother has gone through," though she never provided more information and, being true to the family code, I never asked.

Mother kept her spirits up through back room conversations with co-workers at the library, laughing to ease each other's burdens: frustrations with husbands and in-laws, children's bicycle accidents and illnesses. When she walked through the stacks shelving books or sat at the reserved book desk, she was serious and strictly quiet, but in the back room filling out forms and ordering books, my mother chatted happily for hours. She belonged to a rare genotype—extroverted librarian.

As my father found his way into the underground gay society on campus, their independence was emotionally essential. My father starting asking everyone to call him Mac, because it became confusing to have one name at home and the other at the university. He was extremely busy completing a master's degree in psychology, and then he took a new job in the Registrar's Office.

As assistant to the registrar, one of Mac's jobs was to teach faculty to complete grade reports in a timely fashion. These handwritten reports on manila card stock piled up on his desk at the semester's end. He cursed this mundane and overly detailed job for several weeks at the end of every term. He arrived home later than usual and poured an extra shot over the rocks in his manhattan. In his negative and moody periods, he'd mumble at Marsha and me over simple things, like leaving our shoes on the stairs again, so we scattered to our rooms like bugs when lights go on, to be safe when he came up the back stairs.

He told Mom, "Professors have lousy handwriting. . . . Why, you'd think they'd all gone to medical school. They check the boxes incorrectly and give their students way too much leeway to turn in overdue papers—then end up running their reports over to our office at the very last minute." It drove him nuts, he said. In frustration, he asked for permission to be on the program agenda for faculty orientations whenever possible. That way, a majority of faculty could hear his ideas for swifter and more efficient grading procedures and have a person to feel obliged to when the quarter ended. It's possible that Walther sat in the audience as Mac dryly gave his five-minute presentation on the evils of overdue grade reports. Maybe he noticed Walther smiling at the one carefully placed joke he offered at the end of the speech, so they would find him approachable if not downright amiable when they had to call him at midnight with a problem.

"And don't expect me to come pick up your grade reports in person," he said. "We considered hiring a Bernese mountain dog to collect them, but no one wanted to take him home at night." His theater experience came in handy but was underappreciated by his audience. Except, perhaps, for Walther. When he finished his joke, he wrote his phone numbers on the chalkboard behind him, both his work number and then, while adding his home number, he told them, "You may only call me at this number in the twenty-four hours before we go to press with your reports." Social boundaries were still respected in the early sixties; I shudder to think what it might have been like if they could have sent him texts. Walther, who usually worked ahead rather than behind, nevertheless took out his pen and wrote down both numbers. It would be a while before he would call.

We were all on our own journeys, held together by the brick and mortar that surrounded us, along with respect and loyalty. Following Mom and Dad's patterns, my sister and I orbited around each other until adulthood.

My sister was obliged to keep me company in childhood, a job she resented. To escape from her tagalong sister, she created a conspiratorial sisterhood. Marsha befriended Rita Jean, who lived in the yellow house next door. Rita Jean had a cow-girl-style, rugged survival instinct; she was all limbs, which were usually scraped raw or scabbing over. She came into the world a ringleader. She led my emotionally timid sister on exciting adventures and, in return, commanded her loyalty. To them, I was the kid they could bribe, cajole, snitch on, threaten, and abandon.

When I was so young that mother's pencil marks on the wall indicating my height hadn't yet reached the top of her yardstick, we awoke on a Saturday morning to see massive snow drifts in the yard. Marsha and I whined like enthusiastic puppies to go outside. The landscape sparkled, and melting snow globs hung precariously on tree branches overhead. Rita Jean was in her front yard, carving out snow angels. As Marsha raced out the front door, my mother sternly called to her.

"Wait! Let me finish getting Karen's mittens on, and you must take her with you. No snowball fights with her, right? She's too small for that. . . . I'll keep an eye out for you."

She frequently promised to be watching, even warning us, "I have eyes in the back of my head."

Marsha knew Mother would become distracted in the kitchen, cooking, washing up, or sitting down to sip hot coffee and have a smoke. So Marsha trudged out the front door with me in tow, and when we were out of Mom's sight, she took off toward Rita Jean's house, leaving me stuck in a snowdrift. I hollered till my lungs ached, which eventually alerted Mother. The front door flew open.

"Hey, Karen, where is your sister?"

"I don't know!" I blubbered.

"Oh, alright, I'm coming. . . ."

Mother rescued me repeatedly as Marsha's peers pressured her to "dump the kid." The story repeated itself in different ways as we grew older. Marsha and Rita Jean put old sheets on the ends of brooms and waved them outside my bedroom window at night, leaving me with ghostly nightmares.

On balmy firefly-lit summer evenings, our neighborhood gang played flashlight tag. The person who was "it" leaned against our large trees, flashlight turned off in the dark while everyone hid. After counting to some ungodly number like fifty, the person who was "it" could turn on the light and go looking. Nose in the dirt, hiding under low bushes, I used my size to my advantage. In my secret place, I had a viewpoint from which to watch the risk takers race from spot to spot to outrun the light's beam—until Rita Jean discovered my spot alongside her house. With her flashlight glaring in my eyes, I crawled out and became "it." Leaning against the counting tree, shouting "twenty-one," "twenty-two," "twenty-five," on and on I droned while Marsha, Rita Jean, and about a dozen other kids conspired to end the game. Instead of hiding, they all went home, leaving me to search without finding anyone for nearly an hour. My sister went home with Rita Jean, who had an invisible mother like the ones in Peanuts cartoons. Mom didn't know what had happened until, in exasperation, I went into the house crying and once more fell into her arms.

The four-year difference between my sister and me set us worlds apart, and we looked funny side by side. "Mutt and Jeff" Father called us, after cartoon characters. While Marsha grew taller and wider, I remained skinny. I was often told that I "ate like a bird," furthering the distance between us by early adolescence. We fought territorial battles over makeup and curlers in our shared bathroom, and we fought over which radio station Mom should play in her new Rambler.

Things shifted slightly once my sister started doing pre-teen things she wasn't supposed to and needed me on her side. "Don't tell Mom that I'm having Rita Jean over when they go out to dinner," or "Don't tell Mom that some friends are coming over tonight while they're at dance club." I could keep a secret; hey, I had been trained by the best. And this is how I won her over.

Chapter 18

No One Dives Deep

"You're cheating again," I whined.

Marsha elbowed me a good one.

"Okay, girls, that's enough," Mom said, and she was the disciplinarian, so we listened for about fifteen seconds. When we resumed poking each other, my father supported Mom with a low growl, "Girrrrrlllls."

My sister and I relentlessly teased each other in the back seat of our 1956 Chevy Bel Air on the day-long trip from Columbus, Ohio, to see the Watts Bar Dam on the Tennessee River. Mom passed a road-trip survival kit into the back seat, handing us both Auto Bingo and Traffic Safety Bingo Cards made of sturdy cardboard with pictures of things you could see out your car window and sliding translucent orange plastic doors to cover them. The Traffic Safety Card had signals and signs on it and was the harder of the two. I preferred the Auto Bingo game. I spotted dogs, stoplights, benches, fireplugs, tow trucks, and fruit stands to build up my score. As in all bingo, either a single line or the whole card won the game.

I was still willing to do "kids' stuff," but my sister was too old for such games. She just waited until I spied things and checked them off her game board. She had the new issue of *Teen Magazine* on her lap and was consumed with a story about Brenda Lee. It pissed me off that she claimed to win Auto Bingo sometimes without even looking up, but whining got me nothing other than Mother's left arm thrown across the back of her seat and a swat on the knee. "Enough," she said. I'd heard it a million times. I rolled my eyes and leaned against the door and pouted for the next fifty miles. And when I could no longer see the scenery out the window in the growing darkness, I fell asleep.

I can't actually say I was excited to be going on a family vacation, because this was our first, and I didn't know what to expect. Dad's insurance agent and close friend Bob Murray drummed up this vacation for our families to share. We all met at a run-down resort, in the height of the muggy August mosquito season. A series of cabins with kitchens were built helter-skelter around a common lawn and small kidney-shaped pool. The adults gathered poolside with a cooler, an abundance of white hotel towels, glasses of ice and booze, packs of Pall Malls, and snacks from vending machines.

For a week, Marsha and I were saddled with the Murray children, who were adopted, which Mother prejudicially said explained everything about them. Suzie was a lanky pre-teen, awkward as a giraffe in infancy, dark haired, with piercing brown eyes usually focused on the ground, but occasionally lifted to swat a mosquito or glare at her brother. Brian was extremely shy and socially off-kilter. At fifteen, he withdrew into himself so far no one could find him. He just circled our activities like a silent planet. Since in our family we weren't allowed to say anything bad about anyone, we had what I later understood to be code words we used in these circumstances. The Murray children, we would say, were "odd," and following a mandate by Mother to "just get along," that's what we did.

By halfway through the week, the Murray children pretty much stayed in their cabin room, and Marsha, in her adult avoidance stage of development, joined them for unending games of Monopoly. This also allowed her to avoid putting on her bathing suit and feeling awkward about her changing body. She had not lost weight as she had hoped by growing taller. She was having a rocky go of adolescence, and the *Teen Magazine* story about how you can "look slimmer in minutes without a diet" didn't help. So, I took my skinny body in a lime green one-piece suit with matching plastic sandals and flip-flapped my way to the pool.

Stirring cocktails and lounging on metal chairs padded with damp towels, the adults were in full swing. Mom leaned in and told Bob an "off color" joke about a double-crossing insurance salesman, knowing he'd repeat it to his friends. Bob's wife, Frances, and the only tell-all friend my mother ever had, reapplied her lipstick and patted down her jet black hair, commenting on the relentless heat and their good fortune at having cold gin in the ice chest.

Sitting on the edge of the pool, I noticed that the aquamarine paint was peeling off its underbelly. Gritty concrete pebbles pressed into my bathing-suited buttocks and bare thighs. Dripping wet with sweat, desperate to get some relief, I felt my head pounding from tension and the thick chlorine smell. I'd grown out of scary nightmares, closet monsters, interlopers under beds, but I could still feel my skin crawl. The pool water's surface reflected a cluster of bright white Tennessee clouds that passed quickly over it, but the water was also home to fast, nearly invisible spiders.

I ached with longing to dive deep, but coming up would have put it all at risk. Diving in would rinse them off, but coming up, these tiny nemeses would cover my head and shoulders like a veil I could not pull off in one fell swoop. In this tension between the desire for the cool relief of a summer swim and the possibility that I might emerge in a cloak of terror, I sat alone and silent.

For the first time in my life, I saw my father's skinny legs from the ground up, and I wished he'd get in the pool to protect me. Instead he got the skimmer tool and walked around the pool a few times.

"Hey, Dad," I was still creeped out. "Thanks, would you get in with me?"

Everyone looked at him.

"Honey, you know I hate swimming—maybe later."

I knew what "maybe later" meant—never. He sat back down, sipped his drink and shrugged his shoulders. We all sat in silence for a while, staring at the pool, still churned up by skittish bugs. Actually, no one in our family dove deep; we all skimmed the surface, despite the sweat and the relentless humidity. Mom laughed, sipped her manhattan, dragged on her cigarette, and broke the silence with another funny story. But none of us dove in.

Years later, I began a career in which I could rebel against my family's honesty avoidance. With colleagues and close friends I even called myself "an intimacy junkie." In pastoral ministry, there are few boundaries and abundant personal connections. People came into my office and said, "I never told anyone this before, but . . . ," and I was the one who got to hear it, got to know the soul of another person struggling for wholeness. Young couples talked about their fears going into marriage, and older couples talked of the challenges of sexual intimacy. A social worker knocked on my office door one day and asked me to tell a twelve-year-old whose father was in jail that her mother had plunged off a mountainside in her Toyota station wagon and been killed instantly. Sitting at the bedside of older dying parishioners felt like precious time, where guilt and forgiveness, regrets and accomplishments flowed easily in our conversations. I found that other people could talk candidly about their lives with little or no shame, and being with them was richly rewarding. I became good at listening to other people's truths.

And gradually I found the ability to speak my own truth. In seminary, we were taught to leave our own stories out of our sermons, so my preaching was flat and lifeless. Eventually I grasped the art of telling my own story as a way to inspire and connect to universal human conditions. Like any kid with a new skill, I even erred on the side of too much truth and received an evaluation one year that read, "We like her candor, but she lacks tact." I was still developing the ability to speak the truth *with love* as I watched people around me find freedom through confession and connection.

Over time, I learned that there are spiders on the surfaces of all our lives, but we miss too much when we just sit at the pool's edge. There's a story about Jesus going to Bethesda for a spa day and encountering a sick person who was waiting for someone else to lower him into the healing waters at just the right time for a miracle to happen. Jesus knew the man's weakness and said to him, "Do you want to be made well?" The man nodded. "Then take up your pallet and walk." In other words, don't get stuck by the side of the pool. The man gained his health by walking away, and I gained mine by diving deep.

Chapter 19

The Columbus Gallery of Fine Arts

When I was in middle school and my sister, Marsha, was sailing the rough waters of teenaged romance, our father fell in love. I am certain on this point, thought I can't verify the exact day it happened. I am using historical fragments the way an archaeologist glues a pot together, one shard at a time.

The Columbus Art Museum opened a new exhibit called *Sixteen German Artists* in 1963. After a lecture about the paintings, Mac walked slowly toward the reception area, and in doing this, glanced across the room at two men sitting and talking at the back of the hall. Doug Gould from the Theater Arts Department at the university passionately gestured as he spoke—amusing his friend Walther, who sat next to him. Walther stretched his arm across an empty seat and looked around the room, his nervousness evident in one crossed leg that bounced rhythmically. They waited for the crowd to clear. When Walther leaned over and muttered something to Doug, Mac didn't catch the content, but he heard Walther's German inflection and slightly guttural speech. *He'll make my mother happy when I bring him home for dinner,* he laughed to himself, *—as if I could.*

Walther joined the faculty at Ohio State University the year I was five. He had earned a BS degree, *magna cum laude,* at Columbia

WALTHER P. MICHAEL   "MAC" McCLINTOCK

University, where he continued his studies. He worked on a National Economics Research Project for four years and arrived in Columbus ABD (all but dissertation) to become an economics instructor. He specialized in the field he first explored in Frankfurt, international economies and trade. He brought book boxes and a few personal treasures he'd collected along the way and moved into an apartment on High Street. A mutual friend planned to introduce him to Mac.

Mac made his way to the buffet table and scooped up a small crustless white bread, cucumber, and cream cheese sandwich. He didn't turn his back for long. He was enthralled by the man Doug had planned to introduce to him that evening. Was it the accent, the tilt of Walther's head, or his easy conversational banter? Mac's intensely shy manner often tripped him up, and it annoyed him at this moment. He wanted to walk up to them and extend a hand, but his feet felt like dumbbells against the floor. A waiter waved a champagne glass under his nose—not his favorite drink, but if he drank it quickly it could loosen him up a bit, so he took it. He disappeared into the crowd but kept his eye on them. Doug tapped Walther on the shoulder, and they arose and headed in Mac's direction.

"Hello, old friend." Doug clapped him around the shoulder. "Mac, this is the man I've been telling you about; Walther meet Mac," he said casually and headed to the drink bar.

Walther reached out his hand and Mac had no willpower over his body at that moment. In all his years he had never been thunderstruck like this, and the sudden emotional rush destabilized him. *Just say something.*

"Doug and I share a passion for theater, but I work in the registrar's office."

"I know." This puzzled Mac. "I attended one of your recent lectures on the moral lassitude of professors when it comes to turning in grade reports." He grinned warmly.

"Oh, God, those bits are not my finest performances."

"And you freely gave your home phone number away. . . . I wrote it down."

An awkward silence followed. Mac knew that Doug had told Walther about his "situation" at home. But he didn't know what to say about it, so he changed the subject.

"Doug tells me you're in the economics department and finishing your dissertation. How's that going?"

"International capital movements bore most people to tears." He rolled his eyes.

Mac willed himself to stay focused on the conversation, since he was both present and observing himself from some faraway camera angle.

"Well, then, I could bore you to tears with student records." Blushing, he looked briefly at the ceiling and then back to Walther to make eye contact. They were doing the flirtation dance with every step met by the other giving permission to continue. Mac liked hearing his voice.

"My mother was German," Mac said.

"Funny, my mother was German, too." Laughter passed between them effortlessly.

"Do you know the language?" Walther asked.

"I can understand a few words and phrases, but I can't speak it. I own a few German language lessons recorded on wax cylinders we play on an old Edison phonograph. My mother acculturated so quickly that none of it passed down to me."

"*Wie geht es Ihnen heute Abend?* Walther asked and quickly added, "How are you tonight?""

"*Gut danke* . . . but that's really my limit. I wish I could speak it; seems a shame that I missed out on the chance to know two languages as a child. Do you speak other languages?"

"French, Italian, Portuguese if I'm drunk enough, though it slurs into Spanish rather quickly. Once you have one romance language down, you can fake your way through the others."

Mac watched his lips and studied his brown hair dusted with a few gray hairs giving him dignity, smiled at his prominent ears. He forced himself to take a step backward, hoping to briefly disrupt the gravity that pulled him in Walther's direction.

Thinking logically, this moment might have been conflicting for my father. He had Alice at home, and two adolescents can be a handful. But perhaps he had prepared for this day, for falling in love, even welcomed it, yearned for something so much deeper than his friendship with my mother. Prayed for this moment while lying next to Alice the night before as they consoled each other about how sad it was that their love had not fully formed and fell asleep together. Life provides us with too few opportunities to love deeply, too few safe attachments, too few people who believe wholeheartedly in our divinity. Until Walther stepped onto the stage of his life, there had not been anyone whose arms were safe enough to hold his free fall. Until Walther, he had stood alone while studying the art museum's paintings, taking longer than it takes to read the sign. No one before Walther brought the world to his doorstep or understood the way that being gay gnawed at him. He had prepared for this moment, without knowing when or where or with whom it would happen.

After a volunteer came by and filled their champagne glasses, Mac teased Walther a little.

"So you're an expert in romance languages."

"Ah, but real romance . . . not my strong suit; I'm so practical really, known to my friends and family as 'a confirmed bachelor.'" And there was the clue, the term people used in order to avoid saying, "I'm gay," while at the same time saying it.

"The only person who comes to my house is my secretary, cook, and housekeeper Velma Blue—a sweetheart who thinks I am Lawrence of Arabia. She threatens to write a book about me."

My father, the muse, reminds me that I have now saved Velma from having to write a book because I have included Walther in this one. He tells me that at this moment he and Walther would have gone before any judge, or walked up any old church aisle arm in arm and pronounced their intent to marry—if this moment had come fifty years later. He doesn't say if they left in one car or two, or set a lunch date instead. Those are small details in the bigger story that says this moment changed everything.

I am oddly happy for them both. Possibly my mother was even happy for them at the start. She'd no longer wonder when or where this would inevitably happen. It was far safer for him to be with Walther than out on a search into unseemly one-night stands. He could reassure her that he was going to stay with her, that he wouldn't move out or start over. She could put an end to wondering if he'd change or if the problem had been the way she was sexually unappealing.

Perhaps she saw the look on his face that very night when he skipped up the long staircase from the garage to the living room, could feel it in the air that surrounded him, in the way he stood even taller than usual, as he flung his hat up onto the high shelf in the closet instead of neatly placing it there and straightening the stack. . . . She could see these little signs that love had overcome him. *He hadn't looked that way for a very long time, if ever,* she thought to herself. And she was happy for him and lonely for him all at the same time.

Chapter 20

Our New Basement

The year I turned ten, we moved into a split-level house built of concrete blocks with gray siding. Mom and Dad needed more space between them. Our first home had been small and gave us plenty of places to play together; the new one was large enough for everyone to have a room to retreat to. Going from the main living level to the basement took exactly twenty-nine steps, with the air steadily growing colder as we descended into the dark earth. Mom, Dad, Marsha, and I lived in the rest of the house, but when we entered the basement, we were guests in Dad's domain.

The basement served as a tornado shelter in the spring and kept the house cool in the summer. It was dreadfully cold in the winter. Rough gobs of mortar had oozed down the walls like pus from a wound and hardened in place. On sunny days, natural light peeked in from two window wells just beneath the ceiling. In a corner under the stairs, the laundry area smelled of dryer sheets, Mother's perfume, and cigarette smoke. When my sister had to get her laundry from the basement, she begged, "Oh, please, don't make me go to the dungeon." My mother sarcastically referred to this area as "your father's cave."

A workbench along one side of the room was as wide as the upstairs living room. Pegboards hung with tools lined both side walls. An old cherry dresser in which Dad stored his paintbrushes stood proudly. After a flood cascaded into our basement, the dresser was the lone survivor. Dad rescued it and restored it by rubbing away every water line with linseed oil, using his patient bare hands.

Floor-to-ceiling metal shelves divided the room in half. The back half stored Dad's old army footlocker, broken dining chairs he intended to fix, and highchairs awaiting grandchildren. Items ordinary people would discard, Dad salvaged. He wired old vases and turned them into lamps and salvaged other people's lumber to make stand-up figures of old-fashioned carolers for the front lawn at Christmas. I was ready to be rid of the plaster cast I had worn when I broke my leg, but the brightly penned signatures and scribbles reminded Dad of some modern artwork. After the technician cut me out of that old cast, Dad hung it on the wall.

Dad was more a collector than a hoarder. He kept *National Geographic* magazines, arranged by date, in upright cardboard boxes, along with *Life* magazines from significant moments in history. My librarian mother knew the folly of this. "Once a week, some old guy dies, and his widow brings in his whole collection of *National Geographic* magazines," she told him. "They're a dime a dozen." He kept them anyway.

The old Lionel train's fifteen cars plus the engine and the red caboose were packed in neatly labeled boxes. They appeared above ground every year on the twentieth of December. While the family put up and decorated the Christmas tree, the train waited patiently to be laid around the tree skirt at the very end of the night. Over the years, we added little plastic people to the scene. One New Year's Eve, my parents' drunken friends lay on the floor hooting, "Choo, choo," and repeatedly sent it for spins around the track, roaring with laughter when it jumped the rails or ran over the conductor. New Year's Day, we packed it up to resume its place in the basement next to lamp shades covered in dry-cleaner bags, a broken wooden train set, and Mother's porcelain doll, which had no clothes and whose head popped off easily.

One spring when Dad decided to clean out the basement, my sister and I joined him for a while. "I'm sorry to say that the original horn is missing," he said as he unearthed an old Edison that played wax cylinders. So he attached a shiny new horn to the square wooden base. "I bought this one secondhand." On the cylinder's cardboard cases, the Edison Laboratory (1904) claimed that their "Gold Molded Records echo all over the world." We begged him to play them for us.

Listening to the scratchy sounds of a voice lecturing, I asked, "Dad, what is that?"

"It's a German language program." Grandmother Clara could have sorted it out, but I couldn't. He lifted the needle and moved on.

"Let's listen to the other one; I think it has folk songs."

"Aw, Dad, it's a guy whistling," we protested in disappointment. He dug around for more cylinders without success.

"Maybe we can buy a few of these somewhere in an antique shop," he said. "The cool of the basement keeps the wax from melting." By then we were rummaging around for something more interesting.

Next to the Edison, Dad had an old reel-to-reel projector and a box with small spools of eight-millimeter film from Grandma and Grandpa's trips out West. Home movies saved us from unending misery when Dad's tract-bringing brother, my uncle Donald, and his proper holy-roller wife, Aunt Mary Helen, came by after Sunday worship in full evangelistic fervor. They had at least fifteen memorized lectures about living life with Jesus that just didn't suit my family. We rolled our eyes and fidgeted in our chairs as they explained how to get to heaven and conversely how to go to hell. In adolescence, we desperately dodged questions about our activities, for fear some of them were on Don and Mary Helen's list of sins. We went to Presbyterian Sunday school, where we didn't get a list of forbidden activities. If we were on our way to hell, we really didn't want to hear about it. We were polite and followed the adage that children should be seen and not heard. Mom and Dad simply put up with these visits for the sake of family harmony.

At about ten minutes into their spiel, Dad quietly excused himself and went to the basement for the projector. Mom interrupted

Uncle Donald on cue and said to Dad, "Oh, thank you, dear. Let's
see the one about the California coast. I want to go there some day,
don't you?" (When I moved to California she had a chance to see
it.) She leaned toward Mary Helen, who smiled and, as usual, didn't
say anything. Over the years we watched home movies of Grandpa
Chet walking across the OSU campus, looking like Charlie Chaplin.
Everyone laughed. Chet and Clara took annual cross-country trips
once Donald and Dad had enlisted in the military. Posing by every
road sign and river, they waved at the camera with wild enthusiasm.
Travel was both a luxury and a freedom hard-won by Grandpa's
work at the pharmacy. Their antics kept us occupied until Don and
Mary Helen had to go back to church for their evening service.

We liked seeing Grandpa's home movies over and over again, but
we didn't know how to run the projector, and Dad said it was too
complicated, that we could destroy it by even trying. "This is not a
toy!" he'd say when we hovered over the projector, which eventually
remained set up in the basement. "Do not touch it." As was most
often the case, we obeyed this command.

I only recently learned from Duane that after Marsha and I
moved out of the house, my father went down to the basement alone
to watch porn films on that projector. In the 1960s, a series of U.S.
Supreme Court rulings loosened obscenity restrictions. The best-
known gay film, *Boys in the Sand,* came out in 1971, the year I graduated from high school, and preceded the heterosexual film hit *Deep
Throat,* which my seminary media library had a popular clandestine
copy of—"for educational purposes only," according to the label.
Pornography was just beginning to become the industry it is today.

Every month, a magazine in a brown paper cover arrived at our
door, swept away from my curious teen gaze and "hidden" in Dad's
private bedroom upstairs. I found them, of course, in the bottom
of an unlocked file cabinet—both *Playboy* and *Playgirl* magazines.
Where did he hide his stash in the basement, though? Could they
have been behind all of those *National Geographics*? Nothing was
ever locked up in our household. In a family of secrets, how odd it
seems that we never locked file cabinets or interior doors. I don't
even know if our bedroom doors could have been locked. But when

Dad really wanted privacy, he found it in the basement, just some warm clothes and twenty-nine steps away.

Among other secrets in the basement, Dad had a collection of his paintings leaning along one wall, hidden behind a stack of wood and sheetrock. One Christmas, when I was married and living in California, a huge, heavy box arrived in the mail. A silver frame and white mat showed off a watercolor painting of a dairy barn with weather vanes and a dirt road leading to huge wooden doors. I called home immediately. As always, he answered the phone. "Hi, Dad. Dad, wait. Don't pass the phone to Mom." He usually did that, as if I were someone from Mom's bridge club instead of his daughter.

"I got this painting in the mail with your signature on it. It's gorgeous."

"You like it?"

"Of course, I love it!"

"I painted it from a picture Mom and Dad took on an outing to Amish country. The weather vanes are too big, always bothered me."

"Dad, it's great, really, and how come I haven't seen it before?"

"I kept it hidden in the basement," he chuckled.

"Are there more of these?"

"Not really. A few nude sketches. I guess by now I can get those out, no kids to worry about. You can see them when you come home next time."

I paused and smiled at the idea of Dad showing me nudes.

"Well, now, I'll get your mother for you." I heard the phone clunk down on the counter and waited to repeat the conversation with her.

Dad had painted the watercolor of the old barn in college. After the war he returned home, and he gave up this calling when he became domesticated. He never painted on canvas after that. Instead, he used his paintbrushes to refinish things—the mantel clock, the rocking chair, the tongue-and-groove dresser that had once belonged to his grandmother. While he did this work, we were banished to the upstairs. "Fumes," he said. But when he was away at work, we helped Mom with the laundry so that we could see the transformation of these beloved items.

Between Thanksgiving and Christmas, the basement came out of its doldrums and entered the cheerful spirit of the holidays—and so

did his artistic alter ego. Dad posted an invisible welcome sign outside the basement door. We were hired on as elves to work at the
McClintock family Christmas card factory. Dad came alive, designing and executing silkscreen greeting cards. If I promised to be really
good, he'd let me sit on a stool next to him and watch while he
sketched lightly on his drawing pad, then wadded up the paper and
tossed it in the metal trash can next to him.

"Aww, don't throw out that one. I liked that one."

"Karen, you promised to just watch, right?"

He drew a small house with Santa and the reindeer overhead. "I
like that one, Dad."

"Okay, it's yours. It's too little to turn into a card." I made a stack
of rejected drawings on my side of the workbench.

When at last he settled on his picture, he pulled out a box of
Speedball stencil-cutting tools and a sheet of green film rolled up
like the waxed paper Mother used to roll out piecrusts. He cut intri-
cate patterns into the stencil paper. Each year for more than twenty
years, he came up with different designs: Old English carolers, delicate pinecones, forests in the wintery woods, sleighs, Santa's jolly
face, a reindeer in flight, a lamppost with lamplighter on duty, and
candy canes with elaborate red ribbons.

I sat on that stool next to him with my elbows propped on the
workbench until I wobbled and swayed with sleepiness. I got to stay
near him, even on school nights, until he set out the chemicals in silver cans, gathered soft rags from discarded underwear and tee shirts,
and prepared to affix the stencils to the screens. "Go along now,
sweetie. This is the part with the fumes." He kissed me on the forehead and sent me up the stairs.

Most of Dad's card designs required two or three runs through
the silk screen, and each stencil told part of the story. Each time Dad
passed the card through another screen, another more brilliant color
emerged. We were taught to lay them out carefully on long tables
made of old doors and pipes, overlapping them to fit as many as
possible on the tables, but never so close that the ink smudged. He
learned to trust us as we grew older but never gave up his perfec-
tionism. "Watch out! Don't touch the ink," he'd say. "Did you wash
your hands?"

In the month before Christmas, we got a whole year closer to Dad. He called us "his girls." Mom was busy upstairs; it was her job to address envelopes. So that left Marsha and me alone with the crazed genius mixing his concoctions in the basement. We were left to be his co-creators, to smell the ink and his cologne and see him smile—big broad smiles that were so fleeting at other times. As winter days darkened, the basement and my father came alive with light and joy. The old dingy place was transformed, and so were we.

Chapter 21

An Accident Waiting to Happen

My father's parental duties included warning us of danger. Not big disasters like tornadoes or floods. We had the evening news and the local radio to give us fair warning about those. Dad's dire predictions were supposed to protect us from the minor assaults of daily living. He sat in his corner chair reading the *Columbus Journal,* which he could both read and see right through, always alert for impending disasters. Children, he believed, were especially disaster prone.

He grew fretful over us as we became teenagers and more careful about his own words and actions. But in the early years of our lives, when Mother worked evenings at the library, he played with us. I was too young to remember him on the floor with blocks or toys, but my sister's memory fit another gay stereotype.

"Do you remember Dad playing beauty shop on the floor with us?" she asked.

"Nope, I was only a toddler when Mom worked nights," I said.

"She went off to her job as soon as dinner was over and left Dad in charge of us. We went to the living room to watch the evening news and were expected to play quietly with our dolls. But on rare occasions, Dad sat on the living room floor in front of his favorite chair and let me play beauty shop. I'd climb all over him with bobby pins and Mom's curlers, a spray bottle of water, and my black plastic comb and style his hair in all sorts of odd hairdos. He would laugh and joke about each crazy style as though I were the best beautician in town."

"I can picture Dad vamping down a pretend runway in his drag hairdos." We laughed.

"He was free with us then," she said wistfully, "and happy."

We chatted awhile about the loss we felt for him as we grew older and how his anxieties escalated in our teen years. By then everything—including his straight guy disguise, his job, and his marriage with Mom—was in jeopardy.

Passing through the house, I'd overhear him. "Small things can lead to big things," he'd say. Take bare feet, for example. He had a sixth sense when there were bare feet in the vicinity. "You'll stub your big toe," he'd mumble without looking up, even though I felt perfectly safe in the house, which was thickly carpeted. "You're gonna regret it when you splay your toes on a table leg." He sounded as if he were reading a headline aloud. To get outside with bare feet, I had to tiptoe down the steps, round a corner, and sneak past his view across the hall. Just as I grabbed for the back doorknob, I would hear him roar, "Go get your shoes! You could get a bee sting out there."

"Egad, Dad. I'll be careful," I shouted from the kitchen.

"Go up and get some shoes, honey," he'd say sweetly with an undertone of threat. His mixed message was like a dog wagging its tail while emitting a low growl. Not taking any chances, I'd plod back upstairs for my flip-flops, but since he almost never got out of his chair to monitor the backyard, I knew I could kick them off on the back porch steps.

Dad's early warning siren was "That's an accident waiting to happen." "That" might have been a pile of pick-up sticks we'd left in the middle of the living room floor as we rushed to the kitchen for a cookie or a phone call. The accident waiting to happen could also have been a pair of shoes left on the six stairs up to the bedrooms and bathrooms. When we were too tired to go up those stairs, we left things on them for our next trip, which annoyed him to no end. After school, the stairs became cluttered with algebra and geography books, snotty crumpled tissues, and homework assignment pages. Since he wasn't home from work, we thought we could hoist them up later. Even Mom was known to thwart Dad's rule during the day. After shopping, she'd plop down toilet paper rolls, boxes of Kotex, Prell shampoo, and Ajax cleanser within the trip zone. Promptly at five o'clock, since Dad was more punctual than the city bus system and would dependably be home by five thirty, she'd holler, "Clear the stairs! Your dad's on his way home!"

Most artistic endeavors were accidents waiting to happen. Play-Doh could be eaten, leading to an upset tummy. Finger paints could spread beyond the edges of the paper and need mopping up. Crayons were really hazardous when left too long in a sunny window. A melting crayon stained wood, tablecloth, and carpet.

We purchased new carpet in a home makeover just as I started high school and before my sister's wedding. The color of the posh Anso Nylon carpet was rightly named "champagne" and clearly one-upped the old brown shag of our early childhoods. This carpet evoked upward mobility. It was like a soft blanket, and I couldn't help but lie down on it. Abandoning the desk in my room, most evenings I studied facedown in the middle of the living room floor with my books all around. I'd also sit on it while making birthday cards for friends with my stamp collection, colored pens, and glitter. Glitter was definitely an accident waiting to happen. According to Dad, glitter sprinkled accidently onto Anso Nylon carpet shot straight down toward the floor and cut the fine silky threads of the pile, leaving damage visible to the naked eye only years down the road, but it nevertheless assaulted the carpet's integrity.

Roughhousing—now there's an accident waiting to happen, especially if your father collects fine art glass. Dad was extremely proud of his small collection of sculptures from the Blenko Glass Company. Near plentiful natural gas in the little town of Milton, West Virginia, the shop was only a stone's throw away from the town of Ironton, Ohio, where Mother spent her childhood. On trips to visit some remaining relatives, they stopped by the factory and watched as molten forms emerged from brick furnaces to be shaped into fine vases. Dad liked large pieces in mostly oranges and greens that served no purpose other than to look beautiful. During the home makeover, he painted the back wall of a white bookcase olive green as a display backdrop for some of the glass. The taller pieces sat on the mantel above the fireplace. He often paused as he walked by and rearranged them ever so slightly. "There, there," he told a tall orange glass sculpture as it reached toward the ceiling, "you look marvelous." Everyone in the family was strictly forbidden to touch the Blenko; the once-a-month maid was instructed *never* to dust them.

Decorative pillows in flight? Definitely an accident waiting to happen, and eventually one did. Mom and Dad were out to dance club one summer night when my best neighborhood friend, Denise, came over. The Wightman twins, Pat and Mike, were out prowling around the neighborhood, and they decided to drop by. I was not supposed to have any unauthorized guests in the house—especially boys. But they were good Catholic boys, and we were fifteen-year-olds just flirting and laughing, and not even raiding the liquor cabinet.

"Let's have a pillow fight," someone yelled, and before I knew it, the flinging had begun in earnest.

"Hey, everyone, no roughhousing," I yelled in my father's voice.

"Aw, come on, don't be a party pooper," they retorted. I stationed myself at the hearth like a soccer goalie in hopes of protecting the Blenko, which of course drew attention to my position. Mike took aim and heaved a pillow over my head, too high to reach, but placed just right to bounce off the wall and clip the top fluted edge of the orange, swan-like vessel. My world came crashing down as I watched the tallest and most beloved glass sculpture somersaulting in slow motion just beyond my reach toward the new beige carpet. With barely a bounce, the top fourth of the piece snapped off, leaving shards in the carpet and too many pieces to glue back together. The waiting was over. The boys had no idea about the magnitude of this accident, but they knew the party was over, so they took off for home. I walked Denise to the backyard fence, and she patted my arm in sympathy as she said goodbye.

Waiting up for Mom and Dad to return, I admitted to myself that Dad had been right about horseplay and boys. I cannot recall his response, and since he was a man of so few words, his looks alone would have rendered sufficient blows to elicit contrite apologies. I probably cried, which would have softened his heart, and being the gentleman that he was, he may even have consoled me. This is how I want it to have been. My mother's words, "I'm glad no one was hurt," would have consoled us both.

Dad didn't have the power to predict or prevent every disaster. My sister got married while the carpet was fresh and new. Her marriage was a disaster waiting to happen, although we didn't know it then. While working on an art project at the dining room table, which Dad allowed, I knocked over a jar of black India ink, which dripped onto the new beige rug and remained there, an indelible blot on my reputation.

I spent the summer after the Blenko incident painting the back-yard fence, motivated by my urge to do penance for the crime. Dad brought out his Polaroid camera and took pictures of me in my polka dot bikini (yes, really) painting the pickets, which both embarrassed and pleased me. He and Mom took a trip south to the Blenko glass factory in West Virginia in the fall, and he purchased a similar but slightly different orange glass piece to put up on the mantel.

Several disasters didn't happen. I never disfigured a single toe, and no one slipped on the ice at our house, because Dad scraped and salted at each snowfall. I aged out of pick-up sticks, Play-Doh, and glitter before any harm was done. I messed around with one of those charming Catholic boys but in such a way that I did not get pregnant, which would really have been a disaster. But sitting on the backyard lawn one fine summer day, with my tennis shoes on for protection, a bee flew up my baggy shorts and stung my privates.

While Dad didn't have the power to keep all disasters at bay, he did a pretty good job of it. During summer camps in high school, when I was out from under Dad's careful watch, I explored the boundaries of his theory. I came home after my first summer camp with a head-to-toe rash from poison oak (which was the counselor's fault since he burnt off the grasses in our camping area and several of us kids inhaled enough of the smoke to be sent to a nearby hospital). The next year I came home with a cast from toe to thigh after plunging off a cliff. I'd been holding onto a tree atop a sheer dropoff to protect myself from disaster when it lifted up out of the ground, roots and all, and I fell twenty-five feet down a mountainside. Obviously every lesson has nuanced applications, and even my fall pre-vention strategy failed.

My father spent his life avoiding disasters for my mother, Mar-sha, and me. It wasn't in him to leave my mother fending for herself as a single parent on a half-time salary as a librarian. To a kid, a "broken home" would have been the biggest disaster of all.

FORBIDDEN LOVE

Chapter 22

The Faculty Club

1970

I keep trying to fill the gaps in the story. After the war years, my father stopped writing letters and keeping journals. Mother offered short, bitter stories in her grief, many years after the transformation took place. All I can tell you without embellishment is that during my high school years, my straight-guy father grew impatient with pretending.

Mac walked casually across the quad. The hum of a riding mower droned in the distance, and the grasses, newly cut, filled his senses and triggered his allergies. He sneezed and took out his handkerchief without missing a step. The sunlight streamed down, turning up the temperature inside his overcoat. He took off his hat and felt warm from head to toe. At over six feet tall, he appeared to be more confident than he was as he went to meet Walther for lunch.

Walther's international travels and adventures provided endless storytelling lunch dates. At times Mac could see an "old school," Germanic professor side to Walther, but when he relaxed, or was slightly drunk, he had a wickedly wonderful sense of humor. He could revert to being twenty-ish again with the only provocation being a flirtatious handsome waiter with a whiskey sour.

Mac continued to be surprised that Walther was interested in him. Whenever an exhibit changed at the art gallery, they met there, standing before a single painting for an hour as if it were an old friend. Observing a painting, Mac described the way the artist's technique could evoke feelings from viewers. Sometimes they played a game they called "diagnose the people in the portrait," laughing happily as Mac described various mental disorders. At those times, Mac felt he had something to offer Walther—he was less overwhelmed by Walther's intellect. As he first did with Alice, he kept pushing his insecurities away.

He stepped into the faculty club on campus—a mahogany paneled room full of tables carefully set for lunch with fine white linen. Since it was spring break, the room wasn't crowded with professors. They had scattered like mice under floodlights when the semester ended. He put his hat on the shelf above his coat and made his way to a corner seat where he could look out through lead cross-hatched windows. Staring at a clump of daffodils, he imagined them on a page of the Holland's bulb catalogue from which he ordered iris and tulips every year. He didn't see Walther cross the quad or notice him enter the room. But when Walther brushed Mac's shoulder, Mac smiled and turned instinctively. The gesture was casual. Even if others in the room were watching, they would not have noticed the men's unique connection or furtive touch. Nor would they have noticed the way Mac leaned back into Walther's palm, now squarely on his back in more than a collegial hello. They would only have seen him stand to pull out Walther's chair, sit again, and awkwardly fiddle with the daily menu.

Mac had thanked his friend Doug Gold many times over for introducing them. Doug was the first of Mac's lovers at the university, but it had been very casual, and very brief. They had spent an evening together after drinking too many cocktails at a reception for the new dean. Doug had other interests and very little discretion, which Mac required. Doug was further up the authority chain, so the risk of their post-party soiree was part of the erotic allure for both of them. "I'd like to be your friend, Doug," Mac told him, "but I don't want anything more. . . . Next time, don't let me get so drunk, okay?" he said grinning. "I am married, you know." This he said earnestly, although it was his excuse, rather than a moral consideration.

As Walther sat down, Mac thought how lucky he was to have moved beyond Doug and one-night stands, even luckier to have lunches with Walther and hear stories about his travels around the world. They were a more perfect match. Mac's one-half German genetic makeup lined up perfectly with Walther's one hundred percent German looks and serious manner. Mac sighed, recalling the precise moment when he had first felt Walther's outstretched hand.

"They're out of the soup, but the ham sandwich looks reasonable," Mac noted and passed Walther the menu. "I've ordered two iced teas."

Walther paused and reviewed the brief list of items, closed the menu, and said, "Well then, looks like ham it is!"

Mac gestured for the waiter and ordered the special for them both. He always put the lunch on his tab, so that Walther knew it was a date.

"I'm sorry to be late," Walther stammered, still out of breath. "I nearly ran the whole way from the library. The research librarian was on the scent of a quote for my journal article, and she hauled me along at the end of her leash." He paused, "But enough about me, how's your day going?"

Mac flinched at a stabbing pain just above his ear. He rubbed his temple and lied, "Fine." Mac's new boss at the time was younger than he by twenty-five years, and female. Just that morning she pointed out a minor mistake he had made with a student listening nearby. The headache began then and hadn't let up. He imagined himself heading toward the bottom of the food chain at the Registrar's Office. He didn't like to admit it, but he was more and more resistant to change. When Susan asked him to implement her "new" ideas, many of which had been tried and abandoned years earlier, the bubble over his head quipped a few four-letter words he never used publically.

"When do I get to retire?" he asked Walther.

"Not for a while, I'm afraid. We still have the option of taking a trip to New York. There's an exhibit of Dutch masters coming to the Met this summer. Want to come see it with me?" he asked Mac with a huge playful grin, hoping to lift his spirits.

"Of course," Mac smiled as Walther's magic worked. And then softly, he whispered again, as he leaned a bit closer, "Of course."

"Then it's a deal, my friend," Walther reached out for a hand-shake and did not let go until the waiter came across the room with the sandwiches.

"We should get out of town before the situation gets worse." Mac rubbed his cheek to relax the tension in his jaw. "The ROTC building has become home to thirty students with their sleeping bags and backpacks strewn round. It's the hub of their protests."

"Just keep an eye out over there," Walther warned. "It's bad enough that, in the classroom, I have hecklers every day now. It's worse for you in administration. That's where their anger is focused."

"I'm sympathetic—that's the problem. I actually agree with them. This is the most ridiculous damned war a president could ever have dreamed up."

"Do you wear your tie with the peace signs on it to work?" Walther teased, still keeping it light.

"Are you kidding me?" Mac looked down at his overly wide navy blue tie with yellow stripes. Walther took a moment to let his grin widen.

"Mac, face it. You are 'the establishment,' no matter what you wear—you still look like the establishment, right down to your requisition white boxer shorts."

Had you been there, you might not have noticed that they were talking for the sake of hearing each other's voices. You wouldn't have noticed Walther staring at Mac's lips as he spoke or the subtle way they leaned toward each other. You could not have read Walther's mind as it drifted away to thoughts of their embraces and the places he liked kissing. Walther and Mac, at a corner table with a few unknown colleagues seated around the room, just looked like old friends, and when Walther slipped his hand under the fine white table cloth to place it on Mac's thigh, you wouldn't have seen Mac's fingers lock on top of his.

They were carefully disguised, administrator and professor having lunch. That's all it looked like to those who were blinded by ingrained assumptions, and neither Walther nor Mac could risk this relationship looking like anything more. They quickly let go of each other at the approach of Walther's department chairman, Scott Crenshaw. Scott was clueless about the man he called "the old bachelor," having known him for nearly twenty years. He peered at Walther.

"I see you're working on your week off, Walther. I don't know if I should congratulate you for dedication or shame you for not taking time off when you can."

Walther stood to greet him, and they clapped each other on the backs like football players after a great play. Neither Walther nor Mac asked him to sit down and join them at the table, so after an awkward moment, Scott said, "I've ordered something to go, want to get that syllabus done by five today. I've promised Trudy a trip to the cabin this weekend before the new term. She puts up with a lot from me, and this is the least I can do for her. Good to see you again, Mac, is it?"

"Yes, good memory." Mac began to stand up for the proper good-bye, but Scott had turned his back to them and hurried off.

The two slowly took their seats again, letting out air in long sighs, never free from possible exposure. There was a very long pause in the conversation. They finished their meal slowly, deep in thought, sharing their own quiet communion. They were enthralled with each other, happy in silence or in conversation. When they were beside each other, little else mattered.

As lunch drew to a close, Mac resented having to return to work. Walther asked about getting together over the following weekend for a new exhibit at the art museum. Going to the museum, Mac could always avoid having to explain much to Alice, who either found the artwork boring or knew it was their domain and kept quiet. "I'm just not that interested," she'd say.

So they made their plan, as they always did before parting. It was never enough, but they understood the arrangement. Walther had memorized Mac's softly compelling smile, so sneaky it could only be seen at the place where his cheeks met his eyes. Mac was smiling that way toward Walther at that very moment. Walther said nothing while the waiter cleared away the lunch plates, they refused desert, and then Walther leaned in to say simply before they left, "Mac, I love seeing you smile!"

Chapter 23

Student Protests

APRIL 29th, 1970

One night my father didn't arrive home like clockwork. "His five-thirty arrival is one of the few things in life I can count on," Mom said, pacing around the kitchen preparing dinner. "At least when he stays late for grade reports at the end of each quarter, I know he'll be coming home late—and grumpy when he gets here." He had also recently joined a group called "The Last Man's Club," though no amount of research could provide me with clues about this group. American war veterans' clubs existed under that name, but my father wasn't proud of his military service, and by the 1970s, he was wearing leather sandals with peace signs on them. He described the war in Vietnam as "a ridiculous waste of young lives and money." I was in my senior year of high school and had been accepted at several colleges, among them Kent State, which I never attended due to the killing of students by National Guardsmen on that campus a month after the Ohio State University protests.

My hunch is that "The Last Man's Club" was a secret code name between him and Mom for his nights out with Walther or with gay friends. Mom never explained the group to us, but on those nights *she* was grumpy, so I took it upon myself to entertain her with stories about silly girls in glee club, or actors who dropped their lines during my nights in the chorus of *Oklahoma*. It distracted her from her loneliness.

Helping mother with dinner and chatting about the nonsensical details of my day, we noticed the clock move past Dad's predictable arrival time. Mom grew increasingly anxious, because she'd been talking to him about the developing unrest on campus in the preceding week.

"Turn on the news, sweetie," she interrupted my story.

"Okay." I hadn't been talking about anything important anyway.

"That's about all we know at this point." The newscaster interrupted a commercial on pest control to say that the Ohio State University campus was locked down. The TV-4 news truck was on the scene, its bank of floodlights glaring against the backdrop of Bricker Hall, which housed the university president's office and the registrar's office where my father worked. That morning, staff could hear students gathering in front of the building, and by noon, a voice over a megaphone called others to join the protest. They wanted the ROTC program moved off campus. They wanted the university to divest itself of all stock ownership in "implements of war and destruction."

Someone picked up a guitar and began singing, "We Shall Overcome." Others joined in. Finishing the song, he waved his arms to shush them. "Let's have a moment of silence while we remember our brothers and friends who are sloshing through rice paddies in this senseless crusade. Too many have died already. There are students all across this nation joining us in protest of this war, and we will win this battle at home!" The crowd grew larger. And he called out, "We're not afraid, though, right? We are *not* afraid!"

"We are not afraid," they sang, "we are not afraid, we are not afraid today. Oh, deep in my heart, I do believe."

"We shall overcome!" he shouted through a bullhorn, and as more students came, the singing grew louder.

Father anxiously watched out his office window. Even though he sympathized with them, his job that day was to protect the records of the university and the people who worked under him. Some weeks later, he chided himself for not acting quickly and sending everyone home. He reached for the office phone to see if the lines were open and surprisingly heard the dial tone. He punched in the numbers that connected him to Walther's campus office in the economics department. With each ring, his pulse went up a notch, five, six, and seven. No Walther, no Velma. "Take a big breath," he told himself. On eight, he crossed his legs and stretched back in his naugahyde chair, pretending to relax. At nine, and then ten, he told himself that this was a good sign. Walther was likely halfway home by now; maybe his key was already turning in the front door lock.

He hung up the phone and waited for instructions from the top. The administration had had little time for a decision; the building was too quickly surrounded. All they could do was lock the doors. The protestors were not deterred. An angry mob forced the front doors open, ran through the hallways, and sat down arm-in-arm on the floors. All exits were blocked. They demanded to speak with the president; they demanded that he fire everyone on the university's Board of Trustees.

Mother moved methodically to the kitchen and turned off the burner under the stew while I stayed glued to the TV. The commentator spoke nervously, interviewing the head of campus police. The officer unconvincingly claimed that his department along with the National Guard had control of the situation. "We expect this to be resolved soon. We have trained negotiators working with students and faculty to reach a peaceful agreement."

Mother was not convinced and dialed my father's office. The phone line was dead, but she kept calling it anyway. For a while we stared at the phone, willing it to ring. Then she paced the living room. When she finally sat down, she smoked one cigarette after another until she had finished a whole pack. Between drags, she talked aimlessly about the challenges of book orders at her library. Mother voted in every election but avoided political discussions out of a general dislike for conflict. "If my boss would only budget a little more for children's books, we could keep the patrons happy," she said, rubbing out another butt, as if Dad didn't matter at that moment. I stifled my urge to gag her.

At the top of the hour, the news showed riot police marching in lockstep across campus, but we learned nothing about the faculty and staff inside the administration building. When the news finished, sitcoms began. We weren't in the mood to laugh. We wanted news-casters to break in with some good news. We listened in vain for the sound of the garage door opening.

Mother let me skip my homework so that I wouldn't go upstairs to my room. When Dad was away, I had to fill in for him—a job that made me feel both special and trapped. This time Dad wasn't just away on business, off at the Last Man's Club, or hiding up in his room. This time she clung to me even more tightly, but I also needed her. I took out my book of animal poems, *Zoo*, by Ogden Nash. We read them aloud, passing the book between us. Then we played crazy eights.

When the music began for the eleven o'clock news, Mom turned up the volume.

"It appears now that the riot police are withdrawing. Yes, I can see protestors being escorted out of the building without resistance. Some staff members are being escorted by the police to their cars. What a long day they've had. We're supposed to have a report from the chief in just a few minutes. We'll be right back after this commercial break."

Exactly twenty-five minutes later, the garage door roared up and we heard Dad's footsteps on the stairs. He went limp in Mother's arms. I caught his hat as it tumbled toward the floor and flung my body against them in utter relief. We held on. Still wearing his over-coat, he sunk down onto the couch near Mother's spot, where she joined him. She leaned against him while he talked about the day. They were so intent on each other that they forgot about me stand-ing there.

"It's okay now, sweetie." Eventually Mom realized I was standing there. "Give your dad a hug and head off to bed."

Most nights when I hugged him, his body was rigid and resis-tant. This time he leaned toward me, reached out, and gave me a big squeeze. "Goodnight, Daddy," I said, surprising myself. I hadn't called him "Daddy" since I was maybe ten or eleven.

"Goodnight, sweetie." He started to say more. But he paused and gave it up.

MANHATTAN SKYLINE

Chapter 24

The New York
Gay Liberation March

MARCH 1975

The summer I graduated from high school, Duane took my father to the airport, saving Mother the disgrace of seeing the lightness in her husband's step or hearing the happy pitch of his voice. This was the first of more than a dozen weeklong trips Mac and Walther took to New York once their relationship became too expansive for occasional weeknights. Neither of them wanted to risk their jobs, and Dad never wavered on his commitment to his marriage, so they escaped all other obligations and headed for Broadway.

"Your dad's going on a trip to New York in June," Mom said, telling me the schedule while keeping a tight lid on things.

"Mom, aren't you going?"

She hesitated. "I'm not really interested, dear. After a few hours, museums bore me to death, and the shows are overpriced and over-rated. Your father's all nostalgic about the city since he lived there during the war, but it just doesn't appeal to me."

"Who is he going with?"

"Oh, honey, you don't know him; he's a friend from the university."

After she lightheartedly dismissed the topic, we went on to other subjects, which is typically how it went. Until I left home after high school, I never suspected that my father had another relationship. I had learned not to ask what mom called "unnecessary" questions. She wouldn't feel too lonely that week since I'd be home from college for the summer and she'd have me to keep her company.

At the ticket counter, Mac scanned the airport terminal like the sonar screens he'd watched in the army looking for submarines in New York Harbor. He didn't want to see anybody he knew because he would have to explain his trip. This getaway with Walther included several deceptions, but he wasn't in the mood for anything disingenuous once he had the plane in sight on the jetway.

He homed in on the blip on his personal radar screen to find Walther and moved sideways down a crowded row of seats. "Ah, there you are. Hello," he said. Walther rose quickly from his seat, taking both of Mac's hands, leaning near to him, and then hastily wrapping one arm around him. Mac scanned the room for onlookers and patted Walther on the back as if he'd just scored a touchdown. Mac crossed his long legs and pretzeled himself into the seat next to Walther's. They chatted a bit about university news—a new provost, cutbacks in their departments, things they cared about on ordinary days. Mac breathed deeply and felt his shoulders drop into a relaxed place. *We could be any two men off to a conference for work,* he thought, reassuring himself as the agent called them forward for boarding.

For the short flight, Mac brought *The Columbus Journal,* so he could grouse about politics with Walther, and a new exhibit map from the Metropolitan Museum of Art. In his pocket he had a three-by-five card on which he'd written down the confirmation number to a small hotel in Greenwich Village not far from the Stonewall Inn, where just six years earlier, on June 28, 1969, a group of bar patrons had resisted police who used force to arrest them for "disorderly behavior," the State Liquor Authority's term for homosexual acts and intoxication. Tension in the Village had somewhat dissipated by this time, but advocates who continued to seek justice had launched the national gay rights movement. Mac followed this news obsessively. The fear of arrest hovered in the not-too-distant past.

Seeing the New York skyline coming into view, he felt anxious and was reminded that he and Walther should still be careful.

Neither of them had been to a protest march before. They had preferred their own quieter, soul-saving revolution. Every meeting between them put them at risk of losing their jobs and their families, but they found their way around all of the roadblocks in order to visit New York in the year when the Stonewall Riot was commemorated by thousands of people at the Christopher Street Liberation Day march.

In order to get away, Mac had spent the last few weeks of the spring term haranguing professors who hadn't yet turned in their grade reports and finishing statistics for the year. Walther had hurriedly finished all of his students' papers and gotten his grades in on time so they could leave town. Mac was verging on his own liberation, and he could feel the adrenaline of a runner at the start of a race. He could interpret it as anxiety but chose anticipation instead. He pushed his elbow slightly against Walther's chest to awaken him as the plane approached the landing strip. "Almost here," he said tenderly. As the plane touched down, Mac tucked his hand beneath Walther's elbow and into the crook of his arm.

Although I didn't know it at the time, this trip to New York speeded up my father's evolving gay identity. All of his stories were disguised by layers of innuendo. "New York," he told me the following August while I was painting our backyard fence, "leads the country in progressive politics and religion . . . and diversity is everywhere; you can meet all kinds of people there. Everything happens in New York first: movies open, songs hit the charts, and plays are born. If we're lucky, they crawl their way toward the Midwest a few months later."

"Well hey, Dad. I know Mom doesn't want to go there with you, so next year how about taking me?"

"Be careful not to paint the neighbor's bush on the other side of that fence."

"Dad . . . I asked you a question." I exhaled frustration.

"Oh yes, well, maybe someday, sweetie, maybe someday I will take you!"

Mac and Walther's yellow cab stopped in front of a brownstone managed by partners in business and in life, Ted and Ramiro, just off Washington Square Park. Walther tipped the cab driver.

"So good to see you." Ramiro opened the door and greeted them like old, old friends. He waved his arms in the air. "No, no, put those down. You let me get those bags for you. You had a long trip." He handed Walther two keys, grabbed the bags, and led them up three flights of stairs, chatting the whole way without getting breathless at the top. Mac paused on the second floor landing to regulate his heartbeat and used the railing more purposefully during the ascent from the second to third floor. Walther turned the key. "Is there anything else I can get for you?" Ramiro asked. "Oh, don't forget wine and cheese every night from five to seven; too late for tonight, I'm afraid, but I can help you find restaurants in the area—just ask. Now, I leave you to enjoy." He winked at Walther and leaned in for the double-cheek kiss, turned to Mac for the kiss-kiss, too, and took off down the stairs.

"He was too fast for me," said Walther. "I'll tip him tomorrow."

The room was immaculate and the high ceilings expansive, but Mac went straight to the window. "Oh my, the view is always breathtaking." Mac flung open the drapes to see evidence of the fading summer sun in a reddening sky over the rooftops nearby. "I'm ready to see the town, and the town might as well see me!" When he turned back, he was pleasantly surprised. Walther had already changed into his elaborate Chinese robe and was noticeably ready.

Next morning, Walther went to the lobby to see Ramiro for some coffee. He brought one up for Mac and set it aside, then took his cup to the love seat, along with a copy of *Burr,* a book from the American History series by Gore Vidal. It had been on his reading list for a couple of years, as Vidal was becoming a contemporary voice for sexual liberation. This week he would finally have time to read it.

Mac watched Walther for a while without admitting he was awake. *He's so easy to love*, Mac mused, *so, so easy.* As he began to stretch out in the bed, he rubbed the spot on his back that usually hurt in the morning. His right knee clicked into place, and his toes hung over the end of the bed. *Why don't they tell you the hard stuff about growing old?* he thought. With every pain, he worried that his mother's rheumatoid arthritis had been passed down to him. But saying anything would destroy the morning peace Walther had so nicely created. With Alice, he would have said these things aloud and gained sympathy. Thinking about her and wishing he weren't, he roused himself out of bed.

His neatly ironed cotton pajamas lay folded over the back of the chair. *You're looking pale and worn,* he scolded them in his mind, thinking they were nothing like the black silk robe with the red dragon that Walther had purchased in China last year. *I got you at Sears,* he mused, feeling like a suburban square, and hung them in the closet. He pulled his briefs and trousers out of his suitcase along with a sleeveless white tee shirt, put them on, added a short-sleeved cotton shirt, and finished with his oversized Mr. Rogers-style blue cardigan.

Without raising an eye, head still down into his book, Walther said, "Nice seeing you again," in a "good morning" sort of way. He pushed his reading glasses farther up his nose. Mac leaned over the back of the love seat and hugged Walther, who leaned to the left, then right, and they rocked a while that way. Walther put his hands on Mac's arms, and the smell of Mac's skin pleased him. He noticed the shiny gold band on Mac's ring finger. "Time to discard the ring, sweetie," he said. "We're about to have a week all to ourselves . . . decent coffee, excellent art and fabulous love making. Oh, and maybe we should go to the theater—let's see if we can get tickets for a show."

Mac crossed the room to pull something from his wallet. He grabbed up the now tepid coffee and waved two tickets between Walther's nose and his book. Walther grabbed them.

"It's a new show at the Public Theater . . . lots of dancers and music. These tickets sold out on the day I called to get them . . . thanks to *The New Yorker.*"

"*A Chorus Line?* Something more complex than the Rockettes, I hope."

Raising one eyebrow to respond, Mac plopped onto the couch next to him. "Where shall we start for today, then?"

"I have simple needs. . . . I need to find a copy of *The New York Times.* That should tell us more about what's happening in town."

"I recall a good omelet house down the block. Let's go there for breakfast—after a shower."

Walther threw his head back on the couch and smiled.

By the time they left their room, they were famished, but the omelet shop was close by. The food and the atmosphere both pleased them. Pushing a few remnants of his spinach cream cheese omelet aside, Mac thought how many rules he was planning to break on this trip. First, he'd disobey his mother, whose voice now rattled in his brain. *Be sure to eat everything on your plate, dear.* He turned to Walther, "I'm learning to stop eating when I'm full," and set the plate aside. Walther had long ago finished eating and buried his head in the arts section of *The New York Times*.

"Are you up for a visit to Soho this morning?"

"Sure."

"I have some friends with loft galleries I'd love to show you."

Mac waved his ten-dollar bill in the direction of their favorite waiter, Rhonda, sometimes Ron, depending on her/his inclination that day. Rhonda grabbed the cash and waved "bye, bye, darlings" to the customers heading out the door. Walther closed up the *Times* and tucked it under his arm. He tipped Rhonda, who blew him a kiss. "Oh, thank you, sweetie. You boys have fun out there!"

Walther introduced Mac to a few friends who had art studios in Soho, one of whom showed them around the neighborhood. They spent the afternoon analyzing modern art at a small gallery and the evening at *A Chorus Line* at the Public Theater on Broadway.

"One singular sensation, and you can forget the rest," Mac hummed all the way back to their neighborhood. On the walk to their hotel, he was so giddy that he pretended he was in the chorus. He sang, "One thrilling combination—every move that he makes. . . . One smile and suddenly nobody else will do; you know you'll never be lonely with you know who. . . . One, dooo deee, can't remember, all the rest of the song, but the guy is second best to none, son." By the time they were on a quieter side street, Mac's infectious joy got Walther singing, too. He crooned in his raspy voice, "Ooh, sigh, give him your attention."

"Do I really have to mention?" They pointed to one another with six-gun fingers.

"He's the one!"

Turning the corner, they nearly stepped on Ramiro, who was having a smoke on the front steps. "Oh bravo, bravo, sing it again," he said. But of course they couldn't do anything but laugh. He jumped up to let them in.

"Tomorrow, then?"

"You never know what to expect from us tomorrow." Laughing, they took the stairs two at a time to their room.

Early the next morning, tangled up in a drowsy embrace with Walther, Mac took a few minutes to fully awaken and free himself in order to get out of bed. It was Sunday, and he was surprised to have been awakened by the neighborhood garbage truck's squeals, crunches, and clunks. *New Yorkers are obviously not respecters of the religious calendar,* he mused, peeking out the window. *Since it's the day of the pride march, I bet he's getting the job done early to get back across the bridge to Jersey, before he's mobbed by a bunch of queers.* Neither Mac nor Walther wanted to walk in the parade. They were sideline people, albeit curious observers. Mac tried to picture himself in a flamboyant costume and recalled plays he'd been in as the mustached swashbuckler, the effeminate cousin. He imagined his giraffe-sized body in a leopard skin miniskirt, high heels, and bustier, and laughed so hilariously that sleepyhead Walther fully awakened. "I'm sorry," Mac said, but he really wasn't. He wanted Walther to get up and start the day with him.

"Don't apologize. It's wonderful to wake up hearing you laugh. What were you thinking?"

"Only of myself in full drag for the march today, fishnet stockings, high heels—no, boots actually—Nancy Sinatra boots."

"I know a place on Broadway where you can buy them. Let's walk up there later today."

"No harm looking, I suppose."

"There're lots of toys there, too—things you've never seen before."

Mac's curiosity was aroused, but reality caught him.

"I can't bring anything home," he sighed.

"What's a friend for? I'll keep your stash at my house. Velma's the only one who comes by, and she's cleaned every inch of the place, so she knows well enough not to ask."

Mac stared out the window for a moment. "The sun's up and the crowds are already heading to the park. I'm going to run down for lox and bagels and some better coffee, so we can take off as soon as you're ready."

Mac hastily dressed, ran a comb through his hair, put his wallet in his pocket, and took off for the streets. He knew that this parade would be nothing like the ones he experienced at home. He felt poignancy and power in the day, and he and Walther knew they were watching history unfold.

I can only imagine the overwhelming feelings Dad experienced watching thousands of gay men head up Broadway in the New York gay pride march. Maybe he would have laughed seeing floats carrying high-heeled drag queens in gold lamé, enjoyed jugglers in overly tight tights, or just identified with middle-aged men with slightly rounded bellies looking an awful lot like him and Walther. As far away as he was from his parents, wife, and kids back in Ohio, perhaps this felt oddly more like home.

It wouldn't have made any difference what he and Walther did the rest of that week. They could return to see and do more next year, and the year after. Being together so freely and so intimately was a luxury. On Sunday when they boarded the plane for home, Walther withdrew into himself, and Mac was ill at ease.

Mac planned to tell everyone back home about the art museum in detail, but he would not mention the most incredible parade he had ever witnessed. He wouldn't tell anyone that they'd gone to the store with the fashionable stilettos, looked at postcards of men in flagrante delicto, and perused oversized dildos. Or that he bought a few more films to add to his hidden collection in the basement. No one would know that he and Walther loved each other with sweet slow touches and sometimes with vigorous energy, as if they were in their twenties again, ignoring their balding spots and wrinkles.

He planned to say very little upon his return to preserve the family and protect his heart. Being with his truest love just one week out of the year was both wildly erotic and agonizingly limiting. But he recorded and played back in his mind every minute of their week when no one was around to disrupt him with daily responsibilities.

After the trip with Walther, he moved Marsha's old desk and its matching chair out of the upstairs bedroom she no longer occupied. He hauled in a two-drawer file cabinet and his heavy scrolled desk. Over the single bed he hung a 3x4-foot original painting by R. A. Clark, an American expressionist. The painting had the feel of something macabre, dark, yet alluring. The background was striking bold blues. In the foreground, a female nude sat astride a chair, and her paramour glanced nonchalantly over at her. The painting was a gift from Walther, and despite Mother's protestations, he hung it in "his" room. This is where he began living every evening, following two manhattans and dinner with Mother—behind a closed door until it was time for bed. I missed being in the same room with him. After *The Tonight Show*, he'd put on his lackluster Sears cotton pajamas, sigh up air from the bottoms of his feet, and lie down next to Alice.

Chapter 25

Stephanie

I sat on a tall kitchen stool in my sky-blue attic apartment rough-sketching a stage set. I was living off campus near the College of Wooster in the fall of my junior year, working toward a double major in theater and religion. My junior thesis involved directing Archibald MacLeish's play *Job,* which is about a guy tortured by calamity in order to satisfy a debate between God and Beelzebub. It would be on stage at the college in the spring, and so I spent the year pondering the age-old question "Why do bad things happen to good people?" and concluded that the biblical story of Job fell far short of a good answer.

The phone rang, and I reached up to yank it from the wall over the kitchen countertop and heard, "Hi, sweetie."

Mom sounded tight, like her double manhattan hadn't done its job.

"What's up, Mom?" I realized that it'd been a long while since we talked, and I shamed myself for being so busy. She was atypically slow in responding.

"Is something wrong?"

"Well, yes and no." She relied on silver linings. "Your sister has left John for good this time, and she, Karl, and Stephanie have moved in with us for a few months. She's back in her old room; your father had to move out of it. We put a little bed for Karl in there, too. Even though he's walking and talking these days, he still likes to sleep near his mom, and the new baby needs your old room."

My sister had given birth to Stephanie not long after I had left home for the fall semester.

"How's the baby?"

"Well, honey, I didn't tell you this before because I didn't want you to get so scared that you'd never have a baby, but she's not at all well."

"What do you mean, Mom?"

"The doctors say she won't live much past Christmas."

I relocated to the couch to curl up in my lap blanket, stretching the phone cord from the kitchen through the doorway.

"What's wrong with her, Mom?" Sometimes I had to pry information from Mom's lips.

"She has a bad heart and some brain damage. Your sister thinks it's due to John's exposure to Agent Orange over in Vietnam."

Their son, Karl, who was born before the war, was a healthy, active boy at one year, and Grandma's assessment of him was that he was "smart as a whip."

"It'll be really good to see them." I wanted to be there for Marsha, too.

"Well, honey, that's why I called. This is hard to say, but can you stay at school for the break?"

"And not come home for Christmas?" I pleaded.

This violated every rule about home and the way your parents are supposed to take you in. What happened to the mom who always said, "The more the merrier"? I thought about pointing out that Christmastime is one of the few times a year that Dad hangs around with us.

"I just don't want you to see the baby like this, and everyone's pretty sad and depressed about it." I pictured my father dislodged from his hiding place and wandering aimlessly.

"We think you could come home for the weekend before Christmas and a day or two afterward." She didn't leave any space for negotiation. "Couldn't you find some work at school to keep you busy?"

I found a job at the Wooster flower shop, which at first glance seemed like a good way to cheer myself up. But the boss walked me to the back room, handed me a paring knife, and pointed to big buckets of long-stemmed roses he'd pulled out of the cooler. "Your job is to pull the thorns off them," he said, and walked back into the shop. I spent hours with my nose in oversized red roses, often stabbing my fingers till they bled—a banished princess protecting her mother's fairy-tale world. Mom's idea to keep me from feeling blue didn't work. I was blue in Wooster instead of blue at home.

The day before Christmas, the Greyhound bus delivered me to a section of town my parents called "the bad part." I looked out the window as we pulled into the station and strained to see Dad's tall head above the crowd. Wrapped in a wool overcoat and thick scarf, with a felt dress hat covering his thinning hair, he lifted me off the bottom step in a big hug and kept me near him while we waited for my suitcase to be offloaded. On the drive home, he filled me in on the details.

"We'll need you to brighten our moods, sweetie." I loved it when he called me that.

"Sounds like a tall order under the circumstances."

"If anyone can do it, you can." His gaze caught me by surprise. I hadn't expected him to miss me, but at that moment I thought that maybe he did.

"How's everyone else in your life, Dad?" I asked, not knowing that this was a loaded question.

"Everyone's fine" was all he said.

"Got the tree up yet?"

"It's in a bucket in the garage; we wanted to wait till you could help us with it."

"Gladly. Did you bring the train up from the basement?"

"Not yet."

"And how about cards? Did you make cards this year?"

"Nope," he said. "Your mother picked out a nice box of them at the Hallmark store."

Everything that had been Christmas to us was disrupted that year. Because Stephanie came to live and die with us, because Marsha was so depressed to lose a husband and a baby at the same time, because Dad and Mom shared a bed each night without touching each other except for the occasional elbow drift or knee jab. He never made Christmas cards again. It's too hard to be creative in a dark closet.

Knowing a verse in the Psalms, "I hate them with perfect hate," I let myself be angry that Marsha and the baby stole my parents and Grinched away our Christmas. While I slept on the sofa, I had to concede that my parents had their priorities straight. They made room at their inn for the most vulnerable among us. And as I watched the tenderness they offered Stephanie, the notion that a loving God was with us snuck into my heart.

My so-often-awkward and distant father heard Stephanie crying one afternoon, and he took her from my weary sister into the crook of his arm and walked her along the pathway from the kitchen through the dining room into the living room and back to the kitchen in circles until the carpet pile wore thin. Marsha had wrapped the baby's tiny body in soft flannel blankets that Grandma Bata had sewn with satin ribbons around the edges.

We didn't all go to church together that Christmas Eve. I drove myself to the church for the eleven o'clock service while the rest of them stayed home with Karl and the baby. I listened to the preacher tell the story of Jesus' birth to an uprooted mother in a world surrounded by death, and I prayed for my sister. Mom and Dad had become a team for her, and I remained a distant observer at home, under Mother's command to stay detached and avoid the reality that while birth can be beautiful, it can also be tragic. When I left to board the bus back to school, they let me hold Stephanie one last time, and I let myself feel the weight of her body against my chest, fully looking at her in order to say good-bye.

Chapter 26

No Going Back

I would have stayed in Wooster during summer breaks, but the flower shop wasn't hiring. My job as a Columbus Zoo tour guide paid for a whole semester at school, so I reluctantly returned home. I'd grown fond of breathing clean air at college, and my allergies had miraculously improved. When I walked into the house the summer after Stephanie died, I was overwhelmed by the pungent odor of burnt nicotine. It seeped out of the walls as if the house exhaled. On the inhale, it sucked me into the haze of old family dynamics. My mother was still grieving the baby's death and losses she didn't talk about, like her own integrity and her sexual life.

"She cheers up when you're around," Dad told me. "She loves having you home."

While I buffered Mom's sadness, Dad retreated to his reclaimed upstairs hideaway, guilt-free. Dad's relationship with Walther had progressed from infatuation to endearment to full-blown commitment.

I attributed the tension in Mom's voice to the damage of nicotine, but it also resulted from what the courts used to call "the alienation of affection." Their smack-on-the-lips goodbye kiss each morning had changed. Dad now leaned into Mom and barely brushed his lips along her cheek. At the end of the day he often forgot the kiss altogether.

One connection ritual was dutifully and faithfully kept. It started in the kitchen, where Dad mixed their end-of-the-day manhattans in larger and larger glasses, and eventually made two each. Mom put boxed crackers into a bowl and pulled a plastic tub of onion dip from the refrigerator. Then they went to the lime green couch in the living room and sat down next to each other, placing the drinks on a little square tiled table in front of them.

"I'm nearly of age now, you know!" I whined at Mom on the off chance that they'd ask me to join them.

"Yes, dear, we know." The pause was stifling. "With your friends you probably drink, but not in my house. Your dad and I need this time alone together."

She clung to the only connection she had with him. Their once private conversations grew into top-secret deliberations. It wasn't safe to pass through the living room during their chats, and I had to move stealthily from the upstairs bedrooms round the corner to the kitchen. I suppose they could have been talking about Walther.

I was frustrated and hungry by the time we finally sat down to much delayed dinners. One night it surprised me that Dad didn't even thank Mom for the meal, which had been his habit. He picked over his food. "This is the night I go to the Last Man's Club," he said. I was suspicious. He sounded like a friend of mine who told his parents he was going to the library, when in fact he hung out in a bar on campus.

Mom changed the subject. "We have dinner with the Shulmans before Saturday's dance. Is that all right with you?" She shot her "everything's normal" smile my way.

Dad asked, "Where are we going?" She always kept his social calendar.

"Cattleman's, where we all had dinner with Duane and his partner Joe last time Karen was home. That was a nice time, wasn't it, honey?"

I remember feeling incredibly awkward that night, since Dad, Duane, and Joe spoke animatedly about their common experiences at the university—a world Mom and I knew little about. I just kept trying to figure why my parents were hanging out with a gay couple; it just wasn't done back then.

"It was fine, good food."

This time I provided the changeup.

"While you have a good time at dance club on Saturday night, I'll be up at the zoo for our fundraiser, Zoofari, from six till way after midnight. It's my job to keep drunken donors from climbing into animal cages," I told them, saluting my forehead like a good soldier. "We won't wait up for each other, but Mom, I know you'll leave the porch light on." I winked at her and thanked her for the meal.

Dad excused himself to get ready to go out, and I retreated upstairs to my room. Once Dad left the house, Mother made up an excuse to call me downstairs to sit next to her on the couch. We watched *My Favorite Martian, The Flying Nun,* or *Bewitched.*

There's such a fine line between intuitive knowing and actual knowing. Did I know Dad was in an all-consuming relationship with Walther? He walked more lightly. He appeared to be a younger man. His brooding moods disappeared. He spent less time in the basement, more time in the upstairs bedroom I now refer to as "the closet," reading the morning and evening daily newspaper and *Playboy* magazine, which he no longer hid and said that he read "for the articles."

Mom was different, too. She randomly shed tears and went adrift, thinking of days when they were young again and he was at ease with her. She appeared haggard and ashen. Years later, Duane said, "Your mom always seemed bitter and unhappy." I found his lack of empathy irritating, but he was accurate in his depiction. While Mom never entirely fell out of love for my father, in these years she lost the last tidbits of his romantic affection.

Unwilling to unmask him by overtly complaining, she lamented life in general. Some evenings she made herself a manhattan before he came home and invited me to watch the five o'clock news alongside her. It was a trap. She soon turned down the volume to allow for lamentation. "I used to like my work," she said, "but they've cut the library budget so many times that we can't buy new books. I'm left to rearrange the ones we have. The patrons are fussy with us about not getting the latest crime novel for months after the bookstores carry it."

Now that I work as a psychologist, I realize that my mother was my first client. With my sister long gone from the family, living far enough away to avoid all of this, I was left to accompany Mother through her doldrums. Meeting her needs limited my self-discovery. At the time I had absolutely no training, there was no payoff, and I had only my intuition to go by.

Impatient with her whining about a job she used to love, I tried to redirect her attention.

"Mom, you have a lot of friends at work, right?"

"Yes, that helps. And they're sure better than some of my other friends. Did you know that Pearl Shulman drinks so much these days that she's drunk before women's afternoon bridge club?"

"Mom, she usually drives you there, right? Don't drive with her when she's drunk!"

"Oh, I couldn't offend her by doing the driving, and there's no point telling her to postpone drinking. We'll be fine dear."

My mother missed the memo on how this was a disaster waiting to happen. Or she was in so much agony about my dad that she was beyond caring about her own life. If I asked about dance club, Dad's garden, or his work, she engaged in complicated avoidance techniques. While she kept his secrets, she got good at keeping secrets for other people, too, like Pearl's dangerous drinking habits. And she found ways to steer us away from risky topics. My mother was like a killdeer during these years, flapping one wing as if it were broken and luring potential predators away from new eggs hatching in the nest. She knew well how to lead me away from vulnerable subjects too close to the nest. She protected Dad by distraction.

To keep up the appearance of normalcy, my parents maintained social niceties within their peer group: bridge club, dance club, theater nights with friends. Mother immersed herself in sewing projects and historical fiction. She spent more time during the week with Grandma Bata, who was aging and needed help with groceries and doctor visits. When Grandma joined us at the house every Sunday afternoon, it blessedly broke the tension.

Mom, Grandma, and I drove to the local farm market for fresh
fruit and ears of sweet white corn. The sweet sticky bubbles of
apples or peaches overflowing their crusts made everything fine. The
smell of fresh fruit overtook the cigarette smoke. "Sit down here and
let me show you how to get the pit out of that peach," Grandma
said, and I did. "Now what's it like at school?" She asked me ordinary questions that my parents had little emotional energy to ask. I
didn't dare give her the usual "fine," the response I gave to Mom and
Dad, who asked out of obligation rather than interest. She wanted
to know what I was learning, who my friends were, and what my
ballet teacher thought of me. She was especially keen on how I was
keeping up my relationship with God and reviewed the points in her
minister's sermon every week. She wasn't pushy like Dad's brother,
our uncle Donald, but she still brought over little printed poems and
prayers.

Grandma's relationship with Jesus was so solid that I trusted her to
be steady-on in any trial. At her husband Sam's funeral, she didn't
cry a single tear, not by any edict, or for a lack of love, but simply by acceptance. "No point crying now," she said, having cried for
months while he was sick with cancer. "He's gone to be with Jesus."

While Mom sang little ditties, Grandma sang church hymns—
shucking corn and trimming the ends off green beans on summer
days in our kitchen. When I was little, she sang "Jesus Wants Me for
a Sunbeam," "Jesus Loves Me," and "This Little Light of Mine." In
my teens, she sang more complicated songs like "Amazing Grace"
and "Come Thou Fount of Every Blessing." She steered clear of the
maudlin songs and whole collections of hymns about the cross that
we sometimes sang at church. True to her temperament, she picked
uplifting songs.

"On Christ the solid rock, I stand, all other ground is sinking
sand," she sang, and we came in on the next part: "All other ground
is sinking sand."

As my mother's only confidant, Grandma was regularly informed
and updated. Knowing about what she might have called Dad's "ten-
dencies" and being a listening ear for Mother's miseries, Grandma
accepted what she would have called "the whole kit and caboodle."

Whenever she had me alone she'd say, "Your father really loves your mother," even when it didn't fit the picture I was seeing at home. "And she loves him, despite everything else." A long pause ensued. "I just thought you needed to know that." I waited to hear what "everything else" was, but she said nothing more.

My parents traveled to Europe together in the fall of my junior year—an attempt to keep living "as if." They had hatched their trip to Europe years before as they sat poolside with their friends at Watts Bar Dam, or maybe further back, when we girls were small and they dreamt of their years together after the children were raised.

"Let's go to Europe together," Mac might have said. "I've got to see the grand paintings in the Louvre." She had other ideas.

"I want to go to Ireland and find my ancestors."

"We could find the McClintocks' graves in Scotland."

She had a college degree in European history. She was fascinated with family lineage. So when the marriage was still technically intact, although over in earnest, they decided to act "as if" they were still together and went about fulfilling the life they had planned.

Mom and Dad flew to London together. Fascinated by the castles of English kings and their wives, Alice led them to historic sights. At the Tower of London, the guidebook said you could read the words Anne Boleyn allegedly wrote on the tower walls before her execution. Mother identified with rejected queens. She put this site at the top of her "to do" list on the first day of their three-day stop-over. From London, they went on to Paris and saw the little Bohemian jazz clubs where writers penned novels. They spent their days together, and after an early supper, they went back to their hotel. That's the story as Mom told it to us at the time. Maybe she told Bata more, but for me it would still be fifteen years before I learned why the trip to Europe marked the end of "as if."

On a rare day off, Mom and I sat at our usual opposite ends of the eight-foot-long lime green couch. She pulled out her pictures of their vacation with landmarks designated in colored pen beneath each photo. I had to move closer to see them. She had labeled the pages "European Adventure," but most of the pictures were of buildings. "Didn't you do anything fun?" I asked.

Mother could tell an elaborately funny story when prompted, which helped her avoid the truth. "Okay," she said. "You're an adult woman, after all."

"You finally noticed," I teased to break the tension.

"I'll tell you about Beatrice." Beatrice performed at the Follies Bergère. Mom passed me a postcard she had tucked into the album. With a colorful backdrop of twinkling lights, Beatrice sat on an arch-back wooden chair in the center of an old wooden proscenium stage. She had so much makeup on that she could have been anyone's sister or wife underneath. Her body was strategically covered in feathers.

"I'm not kidding you," Mom told me, "Beatrice twirled tassels on her tits in opposite directions, the right one clockwise and the left one counter-clockwise, at the same time! The audience went crazy." Mom was so fascinated by Beatrice's amazing skill that she just couldn't help herself. She said that she had to try it out for herself, so she went to So-Fro fabric store and looked for tassels.

"The clerk was chatty that day," she said, "and she asked me if I was making a table runner."

"And you said?"

"'No, I just need some tassels for—a project I'm working on.' I must have been beet red in the face while I dug out my cash. I sure wasn't going to tell her I was going to stick them on my breasts with cellophane tape!" She laughed. "I felt like I was purchasing a sex toy or a dirty movie."

I couldn't imagine her purchasing those things. Where did my real mom go?

"Well, what happened?" I asked.

"I went home and pulled the shades, and when scotch tape didn't work, I tried that clear packing tape we have in the basement. I put on some salsa music we had for dance lessons and got into the rhythm of it. I could get them going in the same direction pretty well, but I couldn't get them to go in opposite directions no matter how I wiggled."

"I can't believe you did that, Mom, What a kick."

"It can't be done," she said, "can't be done!" She stood up and gyrated her ribs in a little circle, and I mirrored her. We bumped into each other and kept on twirling until we fell over onto each other in laughter.

"It just can't be done," she said nearly crying with laughter.

"If you can't do it, Mom, no one can." I patted her on the back. "That Beatrice must be a fluke of nature!"

We lay next to one another on the floor, still giggling in pure joy. I was a kid again, and she was playing with me, the way she did in happier times. Before she entered the shame-closet with Dad. For a fleeting moment, the funny, authentic, and a brazenly sexy mom showed up. Mom's alter-ego Beatrice taught me a thing or two about shameless-ness.

In order to get a square meal at a reasonable hour, and tired of waiting for their manhattans to take effect, I took a second job working evenings at Houdin's Family Restaurant. I delivered blue-plate specials and swept up saltine cracker crumbs under high chairs. I expanded my work at the zoo to six days a week. Driving the tour bus was a lot more fun than selling tickets at the gate or steering the riverboat up and down the Olentangy River while male visitors made wise cracks about women drivers. The days I drove the bus, I warned zoo patrons about the temperament of the llamas and the danger of the hyenas and directed my passengers in an always-amazed tone of voice: "Look at that black leopard! He's actually spotted, and when the sun hits him just right, you can see the spots." All living creatures have clever ways to disguise themselves.

Lonely for family, I stopped by the zoo nursery over my lunch break to chat with my sister, who was using her expensive nursing degree in a whole new way. Mending her heart after losing her marriage and Stephanie, she focused on the joys of raising Karl and took a job at the Columbus Zoo bottle-feeding zoo gorillas, some of the first to be born in captivity.

"Hey, what're you up to today?" she asked, switching the gorilla from one knee to the other.

"I need to get away from home as soon as possible."

"That bad, huh?"

"At least you've got your freedom." I was looking for pity. "You're not still stuck at home listening to Mom's unending complaints."

Since Coco had finished his bottle, she put him back in the bassinet and came around to offer me part of her lunch.

"It'll be just a few more months," she said, having no idea how tense the situation had become.

"I have to get back to work." I checked my watch.

"Wait." She pulled me into a hug.

I was living in a house I'd grown out of, with people I no longer knew. My father was happier than I had seen him in years. He laughed so easily, laughed while he worked in the garden and intentionally skipped a few steps as he ascended from the basement. And yet, his happiness made little sense to me. If it were the result of work or a newfound hobby, he'd be talking about it. "What has gotten into him?" I asked Mother, who said nothing. Dad was growing younger, and Mom was growing older, and I couldn't figure out why. The atmosphere around me was hazy, like the house when it was full of smoke, and similarly toxic. By then I'd grown used to taking things at face value, but I couldn't get a deep breath.

I grew so tired of living in the house of mystery, with a hidden plot and an invisible character, that I resolved to leave my family home once and for all. One steamy June day I sat on the riverbank that flowed alongside the zoo over my lunch break. I ate my peanut butter and banana sandwich and let the water's gentle rocking soothe me. "Take me away," I begged it. "Take me wherever you are going." I tossed a rock as far as I could throw it. "They can sort out their distaste for each other without my help!" The sound of the river itself and a huge enclosure of angry chattering Gibbons muffled my voice, which came out with more fury than I had anticipated.

"I'm ready to move out of the gray split-level house for good," I said, to the river or perhaps to Jesus. The song "Suzanne" was humming in my head. "And you want to travel with her. . . ." The lyrics made no sense, but I sang them every time I went to this spot. They led me away. The thought that I was also going to leave Ohio floated into my brain without effort or avoidance. I threw the crusts of my sandwich toward the rushing current and watched them swirl their way around a corner to who knows where.

The Great Lakes Colleges Association's arts program in New York City became the current I sailed away on. I had applied back in April, and the acceptance had arrived just before I returned home for the summer. I was hatching my own secret plot, but I wasn't sure I had the courage to pull it off until that moment at the river when I decided to go. Now I just needed my parents to approve and pay for a more expensive semester. My father balked.

"How about going to Germany? There's a low crime rate in Germany." I rejected Germany. "How about France? You could use your French," he pleaded, "and there's a low crime rate in France." I reminded him of my goal to get a combined major in theater and religion.

"A man named Al Carmines is running a theater in a church in Greenwich Village, and a Lutheran church has a theater in an office building in midtown Manhattan. I could do so much there."

He didn't show signs of backing down, so I pressed harder.

"May I remind you that you took me to my first audition at the age of fourteen and sat in the front row for my debut as the beagle in *Toby, the Talking Turtle*? I love the theater now, and it's your fault," I said, begging rather than accusing. "I really want to study in New York."

"As I recall, you fell asleep at Radio City Music Hall," he teased.

"I was only a kid then, Dad, maybe twelve? You can't hold that against me!" He lowered his bifocals and peered over them as I wrapped up my argument. "I'm ready to step up to Broadway, Dad—well, at least to the neighborhood."

The newspaper on his lap slipped off his knees, and he grabbed for it.

"New York is a big, big place, honey, and you're so young. . . ." His voice trailed off in defeat. My father knew the city more intimately than he let on, both its topside and its risqué underbelly, but that was another thing he hadn't told me.

"Okay, so here's the deal; I'll take a self-defense class before I go."

"What does your mother think?" he asked, as always.

"She's all for it. She said, 'Ask your father.'"

We typically played communication-pong.

"If it's okay with her, I'll go along with it."

Jumping up from the couch, my enthusiasm thrust me toward him, but his invisible force field slowed me down. I crept closer. I kissed the top of his head and took in the satisfying smell of Prell shampoo and Gillette shaving cream.

"Thanks, Dad!"

After work those summer evenings, I lay on my trundle bed with stuffed animals long neglected, staring at hot pink flowered wallpaper and the matching drapes my mother had sewn, dreaming of New York. I was twenty and invincible, dismissing my father's warnings, though I kept my promise and took the self-defense class, which came in handy when an exhibitionist exposed himself to me in Central Park that fall.

"Hey, girlie, you wanna see what I have in my coat?" he said, gesturing toward the bushes and then giving me a peek.

Thanks to the class, I was able to keep my sanity and diverted him, casually (I hoped) responding, "No, thanks, I've seen penises before." He walked away.

I actually hadn't seen a single penis before. My father was like a doll with plastic underwear permanently molded on. Like everything having to do with it, he kept his penis hidden from view.

By the end of that summer, Dad had further prepared me for New York. He described his apartment at the Ben Franklin House on the Upper West Side during the war, told me to watch out for and expect cockroaches, and described the chewy aromatic pleasure of a bagel. He'd been there just months before with Walther but said nothing about that trip. He couldn't have explained his recent visit to the city without some awkward moments and the chance that I'd ask him exposing questions.

Packing suitcases in my upstairs bedroom, I noticed that the DayGlo orange and pink wallpaper was fading. My beloved furless stuffed dog Sparky stared blankly over at me. I took down the bulletin board with pictures of friends in short shorts jumping into the air off the neighbor's trampoline and put it in a dresser drawer. I knew that I could never move back in—not permanently. I sorted and tossed out old school notebooks, drawings, and movie tickets. As an early frost turned the leaf tips of our maple tree gold, I said goodbye to Columbus.

Chapter 27

New York Underground

The Upper East Side apartment I shared with three fellow students had two rooms, a closet with a hot plate, and (as Dad predicted) a lot of cockroaches. We posted a sheet of paper on a clipboard near the kitchenette and put hash marks on it as we killed them. By the end of the semester, the page was covered. Dad was right about the deliciousness of New York bagels, too—dark pumpernickel, especially. A little shop between our apartment and the subway emitted the odor of baking rye, caraway seed, and molasses. They were chewy but not impenetrable. The whole world lived in New York, with spicy foods, diverse dialects, and rumbling subways available all night. You could put change in a machine at the last few remaining automats and get a sandwich, and you could eat at an outdoor table even on chilly fall days. It didn't take long for me to love the city as much as Dad did.

My internship semester led me to an off-off-Broadway theater founded by Rev. Al Carmines, housed in Judson Memorial Church on Washington Square Park. Rev. Al was an eccentric theologian who introduced feminist philosophy and queer theory (before it was even called this) to Greenwich Village through the magic of theater. He proclaimed, "If you want to know how to live, go to church. If

REV. PAUL ABELS

you want to know how your life is in its deepest roots, go to the theater." He was brilliant, but he was also self-absorbed, and I needed
a mentor. The menial tasks he gave students who worked for him—
running errands and making coffee for the cast—became monoto-
nous within my first month of internship. So I went across the park
to Washington Square United Methodist Church, where I met a man
with a pixie face, light brown bangs, and a Midwest smile. He con-
veyed my father's aura.

The Reverend Paul M. Abels was a tenacious advocate for oppressed people the world over, particularly in the West Village. On Sunday mornings, he preached a gospel of liberation in the well-worn wood-trimmed sanctuary that was a safe haven for gays and lesbians, people of color, Broadway actors like James Earl Jones, and vagrants. The African American pianist belted out "Leaning on the Everlasting Arms" and other gospel melodies. Arms waved in the air, hips swayed, and songs were shouted from the floor to the balcony and back again. I didn't know church could get that loud!

On the day I met Rev. Abels, he was in the basement of the church among a dozen multiracial political activists—some making posters and printing leaflets saying "power to the people." Rev. Abels had an office on the second floor, but the basement was where he worked helping victims of violence or finding housing for addicts. In the community, they called that place "The Peace Church." I would have taken any menial job to work alongside him, and I was soon put to work folding pamphlets for bulk mailings and calling volunteers to staff tables at rallies.

The Rev. Paul understood oppression personally. He was the first pastor of a mainline protestant church to openly declare his homosexuality, and at that time there were no rules to prevent him from serving a congregation. He came out publically in a Sunday sermon, telling members and visitors that he was, had always been, and would always be, by the grace of God, *gay*. He was more like my father than I knew, since it would still be fifteen years before I grew more certain about Dad's sexual orientation.

Without two nickels to rub together, as Grandpa Chet would say, I spent my twenty-first birthday in New York by going out with friends who were also down to their last pennies. We found an upscale restaurant and ordered one dessert to share and a bottle of wine. The shocked waiter carded me, which I had hoped he would do, so that I could prove my age and show off my birthdate. He gave us a bottle of chablis for free. It could have been very bad wine, but we wouldn't have known nor cared. We were young and free and had just two weeks left before returning to our Midwest homes for holiday traditions. I got home for tree trimming and cookie making, and during the two-week college break, told my family about my

semester in New York, which included the cockroaches, a day at the
Muppet studio with Jim Henson, ballet at Lincoln Center, and the
Broadway musical *Pippin,* about a lost soul trying to find something
of meaning and purpose in his life.

My father was particularly intrigued by Rev. Abels' coming out
story and our work together in the West Village. Unbeknownst to me
at the time, while he was listening to me, he hatched a plan to visit
Rev. Paul on his next trip to New York with Walther. A month later
when he called the church office, he said that Rev. Paul picked up
the phone. I'm guessing that the secretary was on limited hours due
to budget cutbacks.

"I'm Mac McClintock, Rev. Abels. My daughter worked with you
this past fall as a college intern."

"Of course, I hope she is well."

"Yes, thanks, and she's back at Wooster for spring term. I was
wondering if I could drop by and visit you in June when I am coming to New York with my professor friend Walther from Ohio State
University where I work in the registrar's office. We have a place we
like to stay in the Village." This was in-culture language for two men
seeking connections with other gay men in the city.

Without knowing it, I had introduced Rev. Abels, Mac, and Walther to each other—Dad and I were bonding by proxy. As I piece
together some likely scenes from their connection, I wish I had been
there with them. But we were separated once again by his impenetrable secret self.

Using historical records from the mid-seventies, here's my best
guess of how their visit went.

They met at the Oscar Wilde Bookshop, a local mecca for famous
authors and artists. "Here's the important thing," Rev. Paul warned
them. "You don't dare walk up the west side of Eighth Avenue after
dark, because a lot of teenaged bashers hang out there. And avoid
Ninth Street, too. There are decoys walking that way lately, and
when they are approached and harassed by homophobes, other gay
guys in leather and chains jump from their cars and teach them a
lesson in threatening behavior. I don't advise you to go anywhere
near the place. Somebody in the community dies every week. I conduct too many funerals, so much sadness. Sometimes no one in the

family even shows up—only a few friends." Walther and Mac were wide-eyed, taking it all in. "There is a place we could meet on Friday night—Le Jardin on West Eighth for dancing if you'd like to see it. They've just gotten a new sound system. You can count on its being loud and lively. On the weekends male go-go dancers are quite appealing and drag performers are tremendously fun. Shall we go there?"

And they surely said, "Yes!"

Going to a gay bar and disco with a gay clergyman would certainly shift my father's identity and faith—and what they could encompass. He hadn't stepped inside of any church for a few years. He was tired of Christian intolerance and hatred, as embodied by his brother, Donald, and his wife, Mary Helen, who continued to leave tracts on our end tables, warning him about hell fire and damnation. They scared us with pictures of flames consuming the earth and people in torture falling into the pit. On one tract, the word *fornication* was printed boldly across the top. Dad knew exactly what words like *promiscuity* and *fornication* meant—intolerable sexual "deviance." You could go to jail in this lifetime and hell afterward. Gay people have a choice, the pamphlets said, and Charles had tried so long to choose Alice that he knew better. Gays have an "agenda," they said, to make straight children gay; they are all "perverts" and pedophiles, and they are all going to be punished by dying of sexual diseases. He was pretty sure that he fell into one or more categories on Donald's list of the damned until Rev. Abels gave him an alternative view.

I regret that since I had not known the extent of the shame my father bore, I added to it. The only time I ever swore at my father I was fifteen and in my holier-than-everyone-else phase, influenced by Young Life, an evangelical youth mission. It was a sleepy Sunday morning, and Mother was dressed and ready for church, but Dad was still in his PJs, sitting in his corner chair and hiding behind *The Columbus Journal*. He obviously was not planning to come to church, and I wanted to be a family together in the pew, just like always.

"You're obviously not going to church," I said in a snarky tone.

"Nope," he said, without lowering the paper, a bit amused by my melodramatic piety. "Your Mother is going with you."

It angered me. From the top of the stairs I yelled, "Okay, then, we'll go to church, and you can go to hell if you want to!"—words even now I'd like to take back. I didn't understand why he had stopped attending. My words came out like vomit. He didn't deserve shame. No one does. He had done his part in successfully raising me and then given me his place in the pew, third row on the left, two seats in. He never bothered to remove his name from the church rolls, but he had the chance to think differently about God and church when he met Rev. Abels in New York.

In my naiveté, I had pictured my father in the pastor's office, chatting with Rev. Paul about the congregation's justice ministry and discussing Jesus' ethics. But more likely, Rev. Paul urged Mac and Walther to join him in the liberation movement that would eventually lead to the overturn of sodomy laws, establish the rights of gay and lesbian parents to retain custody of their children, and institute marriage equality. Walther and Mac may have spent their evenings talking about joining the uprising, and then faced the realities. With a family to support, Mac couldn't risk losing his job and didn't want to lose the tulips in his flowerbeds at the back of the house, his cocktail hours with Alice, or the chance to watch his girls grow into women. As the liberation movement grew stronger in New York and California, Walther and Mac remained closeted back at home in order to hold on to everything and everyone they loved.

My months in New York and connection with Rev. Ables changed me, too. I accepted what I would call more of a "nudge" to ministry than a full blown "call." Jesus never spoke to me directly, appeared to me in a dream, or turned my water into wine. Yet, what more compelling example of love and grace could I have chosen than this man Jesus, exemplified in the witness of Rev. Paul? He spoke the truth with love; he promised abundant life and joy. He touched the sores of the sick, found the forgotten, and welcomed the outcast. He said that there's enough light in the world that darkness cannot put it out. I joined Jesus and Rev. Paul in action in the basement of the Washington Square Church, where regional church leaders soon thereafter began a lengthy process to remove Rev. Paul's ordination—proclaiming that his sexual orientation was a violation of biblical teaching. He continued to advocate for victims of hate crimes, domestic violence, and drug and alcohol abuse. He was on the ground floor of Affirmation, a national organization of Lesbian, Gay, and Bisexual, Transgendered and Queer or Questioning (LGBTQ) church members. He died of AIDS at the age of fifty-four—too soon for me to thank him.

Gay clergy weren't the only ones being oppressed by the patriarchal church in the seventies. During my semester in New York, I boarded a train at Grand Central Station and rode up the East Coast to visit graduate programs in theology, stopping at several seminaries with stellar reputations. The admissions staff members providing tours were polite and welcoming, but when I met with women who were attending Harvard, Yale, Boston College, and Princeton, we sat in lounges and dorm rooms where they spoke candidly about discrimination in the classrooms, harassment by fellow students, and isolation.

The first wave of women seeking ordination and placement in pastoral ministry were pigeon-holed into traditional roles for women as assistants and teachers in the church. Language references by faculty about clergy were all male, and the sung language of the church in the form of hymns limited the inclusion of women. In one seminary, the graduating class processed into the chapel while the congregation sang "Rise Up, O Men of God." Attempts to broaden the language and role of women were met with fury and the dismissive phrase, "Surely the word men means women and men." As Central American Liberation Theologians proclaimed Christ for the poor and the outcast, women embraced the gospel of the oppressed and began speaking up for their own liberation. I would become part of a larger movement among women who were asking the church to fully include everyone, and to do so I had to go west rather than east—all the way to California to Pacific School of Religion in Berkeley, where women's voices were being heard.

Presbyterians have regional bodies that make decisions about ordination and placement. When I told the regional minister about my plans to become a pastor, he said, "This region has never ordained a woman and we never will."

Presbyterian women graduating from seminaries all across the country struggled to find jobs, or were limited to part-time roles for little pay. While my parents were supportive, my hometown church—the one my mother was so happy to support in its infancy, where their names are still on the charter rolls—denied my "call" to ministry.

Invisibility is one of oppression's disguises.

I bought a light blue Toyota station wagon with Dad's help and loaded it with bedding, notebooks, and a wastebasket full of soap, shampoo, tissues, and toilet paper. Anticipating life in the sun, I left my winter wool coat behind in the family hall closet. As I gave Mom "one last hug" before hitting the road, I could feel a slight tremor in her shoulders, and, stepping into the car, I could see her crying sloppy tears.

Leaving the Ohio Presbyterians behind, too, I joined the United Methodist Church. Methodist clergy serve churches under the appointment of bishops, so, when women and people of color are ordained, they have guaranteed work. The Methodist reform movement intentionally brought groups of people together to care for each other's spiritual lives and reach out to the poor, the imprisoned, and the sick. I graduated from seminary in 1978 and, after serving two churches in four years, I was the twenty-fifth woman ordained to what is called "full membership" in the California/Nevada Conference of the United Methodist Church. My parents flew from Columbus to the ordination ceremony and stayed for a few brief days in the Bay Area.

My father and I had both found a way to live in faith. I stayed inside the traditional church and Father reconciled homosexuality and Christianity outside of the church. Rev. Ables had been a powerful catalyst for both of us. As I walked off the stage area after my ordination service, my father opened his arms to embrace me, leaned his head down toward mine, and said, "I'm so proud of you," for the very first and only time.

Chapter 28

The Pipes Might Freeze

1982

I was living in California experiencing December's relentless rains, so it didn't feel like Christmas was approaching. My daughter, Megan, was just one month old—I had barely adjusted to sleep loss, being on-call at all times, eating for two and nursing—when I invited my parents to come for her first Christmas. I needed my mother's help and my father to smile at my new baby.

Back in Ohio, snow blew up the driveway and drifted against the garage door. Parting the draperies in the living room, my father looked out the front window across the white lawn and calculated about a foot and a half of snow. He sat on the steps near the hall closet and pulled on his rubber overshoes. It was Monday morning, and he had to go to work, so he grabbed the wool hat with earflaps and layered his wool coat over several sweaters. He looked as bulky as he had actually been in the years after he stopped smoking, when he went from 190 pounds to nearly 300. Even though he had dropped down again, there was an even thinner man under there who was looking forward to retirement and the days when he could just stay inside and ignore the snow until it melted away.

He stepped outside through the garage, dared to take a deep breath, and watched the carbon dioxide he exhaled fog up his glasses. He fired up the snow blower he had proudly purchased on sale the previous summer and steered it along the sides of the driveway like an Alaskan musher with a team of huskies. He completed the task in about an hour, shed some layers of clothing, and left for work. He had two more weeks before the vacation, but he was already grumbling to Alice about their upcoming trip, to which he had acquiesced. She had pleaded with him to visit me, my husband, and our baby in California for Christmas, suggesting he'd get a break from the snow and she'd get to see the baby "who's growing up so fast!" Alice's brown eyes, when petitioning his heart, were still convincing.

I waited nervously at the San Francisco airport for their plane to arrive, bouncing Megan on my hip and straining for the sight of them. Mother was all smiles and briefly hugged us, looking around desperately for a place to smoke. While my father and I waited in the luggage area, she went outside to light up. "How was the trip?" I asked Father, shifting Megan onto the other hip.

"Cramped," he said. "You know, my legs are too long for buses and airplanes." He was focused on the steel conveyor belt. He would stay terse like this most of the trip. I asked questions, he answered simply, though I knew he was complex and intelligent.

When Mother returned, she clapped her hands and took Megan, lifting her high in a gesture of offering to the gods. And when Megan cried a little from the unfamiliar face and smell of Grandma Alice, I took her back again. We had a long drive ahead of us, so I advised them to use the bathroom first, and then we climbed in our Ford Bronco and headed up the 101 to Willits.

They were tired from their trip, but Mother and I have learned to chat about nothing when necessary and did so. Megan slept in her car seat in the back next to my father, who smiled each time he looked over at her and just once reached over to feel the smooth skin on the side of her arm. Then he turned his attention out the window to see small towns and vineyards. The hills grew into mountains as we drove north.

Before arriving at the parsonage of the Methodist church where I was pastor, we could see the ranch-style house spread out like fog over a mountaintop, and we could see my husband in the picture window looking for us. Over the next few days, we stayed indoors as rains poured in hard slanted angles toward the house. My mother and my husband were both avid Scrabble players and fiercely competitive, so they kept busy. I tended to the baby. Dad read the newspaper and a journal of psychology he had brought with him, hovering around the periphery of our activities.

On the fourth day of what had been planned to be a two-week visit, he announced over breakfast that he'd be heading home a week early if we could get him to the airport the day after Christmas. He'd call the airlines and rearrange a flight. I looked over at my mother for clues and, as always, found very little there. She prided herself on having what she called "a poker face." Had they talked of this? What did she know, think, and feel? My chest tightened up, and my throat closed. My body knew how to do this, how to be sure I didn't say what I felt. The bubble over my head, in cartoon style, said, *What the @*$#?* The sound of crunching cereal grew unbearable. "Well, sure, Dad, I can take you to the airport," as if that was all there was to it, a contractual arrangement. I couldn't say, "I want to see you as long as I can, I want time to know who you are; I've missed you my whole life." Every time he came near, he would slip away again as soon as he could. Reading a *Winnie the Pooh* story to my daughter, I caught my breath on the line, "How lucky I am to have something that makes saying goodbye so hard." Even though I was an adult and well skilled in interpersonal communication, I couldn't say what I was feeling: "Dad, I always want more."

"I'll drive you to the airport," I said instead.

I looked at Mother's face again and saw only a slight rise in her left eyebrow. So I asked him, "What could you need to do at home this time of year?"

He said, "Well, you know the weather report says the temperatures are dropping again just after Christmas, and I don't want the pipes to freeze." It was a lame excuse, so I made up some bogus reasoning to go along with it. Maybe he was a little depressed, agoraphobic, or anxious. (When you live with puzzle pieces that never fit in the puzzle, you decide that it is emotionally safer to think you are ignorant than to think you are being deceived.) At the time, I had a whiney kid inside me who was slightly desperate for him to want me.

"Couldn't a neighbor check on the house?"

He pulled his chair back from the table, got another cup of coffee, and stood across the room leaning against the counter, so I knew I'd pushed as far as either of us could go.

"I just feel better when I'm back at the house, and your mother will enjoy a longer stay with you."

He passed me over to Mother—as was his pattern: from wet diapers and booboos on my knees to homework and boyfriend problems to driving lessons and phone calls home.

Sometimes he answered the phone. "Hi, Dad," I said my usual, "How are you?"

And as if he had rehearsed his next line a thousand times, "Fine, honey. Let me get your mother."

He was irritatingly flummoxed without her. When I broke my left leg—both bones, clean through—he had to act on his own. After my twenty-five foot plunge off a cliff at summer camp, the staff loaded me into the back seat of a VW Bug and drove me to the nearest hospital. The emergency room charge nurse called our home phone to get permission to give me pain medications and set my leg. Mother was off at bridge club or down at the church, I don't remember where, but my father was the one on the line. He didn't know what to do, he said, could they wait till my mother came home? While I lay on a gurney writhing in pain, he was still hoping to hand over the phone and leave the decisions to my absent mother. He'd traded his family decision-making roles with Mom for his private liberties. While he was numb and silent, in the background I could hear my sister, who was visiting at the house, tell him firmly in her nurse-faces-delusional-patient voice, "Just tell them to treat her!"

Without cell phones, it could have been a long wait for Mother's return. The nurse on my end handed the phone to a doctor to talk sense into him, and my sister kept telling him to authorize treatment, so he eventually did. Whenever I was in pain, though, his instinctual response was to pass the problem to Mother. She atoned for him by substitution.

Mother stayed the week after Christmas, bonding with Megan, listening to my career challenges, beating my husband at Scrabble, reading a novel about Anne Boleyn, and smoking on the back porch. Every puff of that cigarette calmed and soothed her nerves, so she could remain loyal to untruth. She likely knew exactly why he went home, but her poker face served her well.

My father had, of course, returned to Ohio to be with Walther that week and stayed at his apartment, so that the neighbors on our street wouldn't ask questions. Maybe he stopped by our house occasionally, just to be sure the heat was working and the pipes ran free. On New Year's Eve, they surely downed whiskey sours in a neighborhood bar with mirror balls, masks, and friends, and then turned in early for a quieter, private finish.

OUT OF THE CLOSET

MAC

Chapter 29

The Crash

1985

New Year's Eve morning, three years later, Alice was in her groove, grocery shopping and cooking. Mac started his morning at the liquor store and returned home to dust the Blenko glass, straighten pictures, and then hit the high spots, or in his mother's German tongue, *putz* around the house. Old friends would be coming over, bringing food and fond memories from previous years. The liquor flowed freely, the Christmas tree and its little train set were admired, and the party ran into the morning hours. Their aging friends veered from their diets and imbibed youthfully.

This was not a party that Walther attended, nor any of Mac's gay friends. Back door neighbors came, their insurance salesman, the bridge club gang, and dance club friends—all of them historical friends, presumably straight. My father was skilled at code switching. But as he went about his tasks that morning, his thoughts were with Walther, who was off on another adventure. He had booked a last-minute tour from Chile with eight Americans planning to spend forty-eight hours on King George Island in the Antarctic Ocean.

Walther had shown Mac the travel brochure over lunch the week before the trip. The travel company promised that tourists could recapture exciting journeys taken by Sir Francis Drake and other explorers in the South Shetland Islands. On the tour he'd see rare penguins and blue-eyed cormorants, three types of seals, whales, and melting glaciers. The tour included a small vessel navigating "some exquisitely beautiful waterways" and noted that the ice conditions could change the itinerary.

"I'm excited to see a part of the world I've never explored!" Walther said. "The tour falls neatly across the holidays when you're busy with Alice and friends, and I'm usually sulking in my apartment. I thought about going again to see Wolfgang in Texas, but this time I'll go see some endangered penguins."

Mac laughed. "There's nothing exotic in Texas," and added, "I'll miss you, though—whether you were in town or anywhere around the world, I'd miss you."

Mac brought his thoughts back to the living room, straightened books on the shelves, and went to the kitchen to ask Alice for instructions about what to do next. They circled around each other the rest of the day, grabbed an early snack for supper, and mother bathed. She opened her jewelry box and lifted out the silver rose pin Mac had given her on their fortieth anniversary. She pinned it onto her gold-sequined blouse and slipped on black polyester pants. Mac wore his usual gray slacks, pale green shirt, and holiday tie with little green trees and the words "Ho, Ho, Ho!" in red. They postponed their manhattans until eight-thirty, when friends arrived.

Before midnight the crowded house was filled with boisterous laughter, a little singing, and a few serious comments about politics at year's end. Mac played the perfect host, taking coats upstairs and laying them neatly on the bed. He poured drinks and made jokes. Parties became him.

Just for a moment, as the clock neared midnight, Mac found himself weak-kneed and physically shaken, like he'd been punched in the chest. It flashed through his mind that this could be a heart attack, but he didn't have a health history to match his symptoms. *Just sit down a minute,* he thought, easing into an uncomfortable chair at the kitchen table. He felt a little nausea and pledged to stop drinking for the rest of the night. He felt unusually frightened or sad, he couldn't tell which. Pouring a ginger ale in a champagne flute, he rejoined the rest of them, just in time to grab Alice for a kiss and raise his glass to ring in the New Year.

They cleaned up the house the next day, watched the Rose Parade, which he loved, and took it easy. They went to bed early and were awakened soon after when the phone rang. Mac sat up in bed and reached for the headset to let Alice rest. She roused and stirred, overhearing Velma Blue on the line with him.

"Oh, no . . . ," he said, and again, "No!" He fell forward with his right hand over his eyes, sobbing and rocking.

Mom took the receiver, "Velma, this is Alice, what has happened?"

"It's Walther, he's gone; his plane crashed, and no one survived."

"Thank her for calling," Mac said, gasping for air through his sobs.

"Thank you, Velma," Alice said. "We'll stay in touch."

Mac rolled onto his side in a fetal position, and she wrapped herself over him like a blanket. Her embrace was dependably warm, and as her cheek rested alongside his, she could taste his tears.

Thereafter, his days blurred together with grief. He barely slept. A cop pulled him over for running a red light; he was irritable at work and accomplished the bare minimum, delegating tasks to others. Duane took him to lunch and made sure that he ate. That year, Alice lost what little of Mac she still had. He withdrew further into himself, skipping his cocktail hour with her, and staying in his room until long after she had fallen asleep.

2015

When people ask me how I knew my father was gay, I refer to his tryst with Tim, when he was nineteen, as "the smoking gun." That journal entry was evidence that my father was gay before he even knew it, and long before I knew it. But there was more evidence to come. In order to understand my own unraveling love life, I grew more desperate for the truth. For more years than I can pinpoint, there was Walther offstage—shaping my father's personality. Upon hearing about my search for the invisible man in our family, a friend wisely remarked that I had a "phantom father." When grief overwhelmed my father, he was powerless over his own secret.

In my mid-thirties, I began searching in earnest and found nothing. Who was the man whose death broke my father's heart? Twenty
years went by until I asked Duane about Dad's long-term relationship. He said only, "I think his name was Michael." And that didn't
ring true, because Walther's name had stuck with me; it had that
funny German "h" in the middle. I had heard my parents talking
about Walther, casually, like he was no big deal.

One morning after I'd stayed up late writing about my father,
I awakened with a new thought. Perhaps Duane had meant that
"Michael" was Walther's last name. Rushing to my computer, I
googled *Walther Michael,* and up popped a Toledo, Ohio newspaper
report about a plane crash in Antarctica. I sent a text to Marsha,
who found a similar article in *The New York Times.* A few days
later, with help from the Ohio State University archives department,
Walther materialized. We had his curriculum vitae, the story of his
families' immigration, and his obituary.

In the obituary, Father's grief was front-page news. Bill Steiden,
Dispatch staff reporter, interviewed my father, "Charles," for his
January 3, 1986, story about the air crash. It's my father's voice
Steiden pens when he writes that Walther would have chosen to die
on an adventure to dying an ordinary death. "I prefer to accept it
that way," Charles was quoted as saying, but it's Mac who was torn
apart—holding himself together by sheer will. The story described
Charles as a retired university employee and "longtime friend."

How long is longtime?

Could I "out" the man my father loved? I cannot say that my
father and Walther had sex, or that Walther was gay, but I do know
my father's grief, my mother's reports, and all the data adds up.
Finding Walther was like finding a family member who had influenced my life every day throughout high school, college, and into
adulthood. He shaped and changed my father along the way. When
my father began reading journal articles on economics, I couldn't figure out why, because it seemed quirky for him, misplaced. He loved
theater, art, and psychology. Now it made total sense.

They had so much in common: German ancestry, intolerance for
intolerance, fascination with the art world and paintings stolen by
Nazis during the war, service in the war itself. They went to the

Mapplethorpe exhibit in New York, the erotic photography captured from a gay man's viewpoint. Though I know that nothing can be proved in a court of law without substantial evidence, that's not how family systems work. Our family had Walther in the emotional field for a dozen or more years—perhaps my whole childhood.

The archivist sent me Walther's picture. I stared hard at it, willing my memory to grab hold. But I did not recognize him. He looked more ordinary than I had expected him to be; he could have been the guy next door, the bank loan officer, or the man sitting next to me at church. Beneath his German professorial expression lay some other man whom the obituaries described as a more intriguing world traveler.

Walther's curriculum vitae led me to the careers and obituaries of his brothers Wolfgang and Franz and to a story about works of art held by the Behren's Bank in Hamburg that were seized by Nazi soldiers during the war. I was finally meeting the man who had lived in our family under an invisibility cloak. The stirred-up anxious place in my gut settled down as the mystery of Walther was solved.

He was "a keen observer of things and of life in general and had a great knowledge of many things," according to his brother Franz. Walther's colleague Edward J. Ray told the *Lantern* that Walther had "a certain polish and class and a cosmopolitan quality." He was "interesting" the article said, with a "certain European kind of charm and great gentleness." I might have used those exact words to describe my father.

The university held a memorial service for Walther fifteen days after his death. His body was cremated and returned for burial in the family tomb in Freiburg, Germany. Of one thing I am now certain— he left with my father's heart.

Chapter 30

The AIDS Epidemic

In the late 1980s, I carried tissue boxes and candles into a medical clinic in Santa Rosa, California, for a gathering of healthcare professionals on the front lines of the AIDS epidemic. Doctors and nurses were overwhelmed with grief, so we invented rituals to prevent burnout. On Mondays, we posted pictures up on a blackboard—young men who had died in the past week or over the weekend. In no time we had to buy more blackboards. We offered prayers and lit candles to help us say goodbye to as many as three patients every day, sometimes a dozen in a week. As more were diagnosed, the staff buckled under the weight of having to give what amounted to a death sentence to so many vital young men. Most of the patients with HIV and full-blown AIDS were transplants from the middle of the country seeking to find sexual freedom among peers in the communities along the Russian River. When the AIDS epidemic started, fear of infection ran rampant since the Centers for Disease Control still didn't know very much about how it was transmitted, drugs were ineffective, and a positive test for HIV most often meant an inevitable swift death. Isolated from their families, patients relied on the clinic for necessary social services. When they lost their jobs and their insurance ran out, they could not afford medication or home care, but the gay and lesbian community scrambled to find ways to care for them.

I was under the Bishop's appointment to run a hospital chaplaincy program for dozens of hospitals in Sonoma County, and my work with doctors, nurses, and social workers on the front lines treating AIDS patients gave me a place to offer mercy and work for justice. I was instinctively drawn into the culture of my father's gay life. I found gay men incredibly tender and appealing, and I now know that familiarity drew me in.

I worked in tandem with a gay priest named Joseph who was dying of AIDs, the most unpretentious clergyman I had ever encountered. Back home in Ohio, Father had been recently diagnosed with multiple myeloma, and Joseph knew the nearness of his own death, so we talked of our private grief as well as the immense losses around us. We struck up ongoing conversations about the afterlife. Entirely certain that he was going to spend eternity in the arms of Jesus, the gentle priest said, "God isn't going to punish me for my beautiful gayness," he said. "There's a rockin' gay men's chorus of heavenly angels, and I'm planning to join them."

I got the news about Dad's condition via phone call from Mother, who was matter of fact about it. She was ready to do her duty and said that she and Dad had kept their marriage vows "in order to take care of one another in our old age." He wasn't very old—just sixty-two—so cancer preempted his lifeline. He went in for a routine blood draw, and the results caused his doctor's alarm. A bone marrow test confirmed the diagnosis. Dad's bone marrow cancer was crowding out healthy plasma cells that his body needed for protection.

Grief can render an immune system defenseless.

Mom was talking to me in technical terms, her tone flat and distant. "What does this mean, Mom?"

"Honey, he'd gotten the flu and couldn't shake it, and the doctor said that he has a compromised immune system, and his bones are basically dissolving without the power to rebuild themselves."

"Shit."

"I guess you could say that," she said.

"Does this mean chemotherapy, or what?"

"I wish I could tell you that, honey, but we won't know until we see the oncologist in a few weeks."

"Does Marsha know?"

"Yes, you can talk to her; she understands the medical stuff better than I do."

"This is not why you paid her nursing school tuition, Mom."

"I know, honey, but I know you two will help each other get through this."

"And Mom, who's helping you?"

"I haven't told anyone just yet; we want to know more first."

She has a master's degree in library science and an honorary degree in evasive communication, I thought to myself, and noticed the tension in my throat that told me to cut the call short. It wasn't her fault that Dad was sick or that I was some huge number of states and expensive airplane trips away from Ohio.

"Okay, Mom, please take care of yourself and call me after your next visit, okay?"

"Will do, honey, and please don't worry about us; we'll be fine."

They were always "fine" on the surface, and that's the only place she could be at that point, dog paddling furiously to keep from going under.

In my job, I often stood beside the bed of a dying patient, consoling the family. I sat in on meetings with doctors as they explained a diagnosis or reported the results of a surgery that revealed the destructive evidence of cancer. I knew the language of illness that my sister the nurse knew, but I spoke it in the dialect of faith. Yet all of my training and experience fell short as I faced my own father's illness.

One day during a break between visits with patients in the AIDs clinic, I sat side by side with my priest friend Joseph in a tiny exam room.

I confided, "I'm growing surer every year that my father is in the closet, but he dodges my questions."

"And your mother?" he asked. "What does she think?"

"She's in the closet with him," I said gesturing across my lips like I was closing a zipper.

"Does it matter?" he asked gently.

"Yes, and no." I saw his kind eyes piercing into me and continued. "Yes, because there's so much about him I'd like to know. I can't get very close to him with a secret between us. And no, because I love him, plain and simple, just love him."

He calmly straightened the plastic insert in the collar of his black shirt while he considered what to say. I was not literally at confession, but I felt like it. I'd inherited the shame of our secrets, and telling them left me jittery. My legs began shaking uncontrollably. For the first time, I had broken through the force field that protected our family secrets. He laid his hand on my bouncing knee, and I slowly calmed from his warm, kind touch.

"How about this?" he asked. "How about I meet your dad when he and I get to heaven, and we have a chat?"

My tears ran freely, and I grabbed a tissue from the box on the counter by the sink.

"Sure, of course," I said. "Tell him how much I miss him."

"I will."

I wiped my eyes. "I've missed him my whole life."

He leaned in to hold me while I sobbed.

Back home, Mac was referred to an oncologist—a man my sister said was openly gay. "Doc," Mac said at his next visit, Alice at his side, "I know this is going to kill me, but how long will it take?" The specialist's mind raced in a hundred directions, and he resented the fact that his medical school never trained him for these dreadful conversations.

"Well, Mac." He wasn't making eye contact. "I've known some people to live five or six years with this. We'll get you the best chemotherapy and keep you as free from pain as we can."

"Pain? I hadn't even gone there yet; I just want to know on average, what's the average?"

"Well," the oncologist said. "Average? Two years."

"Okay," Mac said. "Let's begin."

My mother wasn't sure if the fluorescent lights were tricking her or if his eyes were tearing up. She couldn't yet think about her own feelings. My father, the one who met deadlines at all costs, be they late-night grades or home to dinner, decided that the two-year average would be exactly what he would get, and it was.

But then Mom got sick, and everyone's plans fell through. She had lived her celibate life, and he had lived his closeted life, thinking that their suffering would be offset by their friendship in their "later years." But later never came.

I'm searching my brain for the moment a phone call came about my mother's cancer diagnosis a year after Dad's. Was I sitting at my office desk at the church, or at home in the evening? Details are instantly obliterated by trauma. Marsha most likely placed the call to me. As a nurse, she was more practiced at giving bad news than my father's oncologist had been. It also shocked me less than the news about Dad, since Mom had told us her whole life that her smoking would kill her.

On a quiet clergy retreat, I sat in the chapel and prayed, which seemed to be the only power I had. I'd picture a healing light surrounding her lungs and shrinking up the encroaching tumors. Her diagnosis was severe—the most rapidly spreading of all cancers. Over the next few months, we learned that it had also invaded her brain. I scrambled to imagine life without my parents—in my mid-thirties, regressing toward age ten. Having a distant father in childhood, I'd always believed that time could bring us closer. I still needed my mother's advice. She whole-heartedly believed in me, and, with my marriage in trouble, I wanted the option my sister had when she divorced—an open reservation at my childhood home.

Chemotherapy tired my mother to the point that she couldn't care for Father at home. "It's okay, Alice," he told her; "I'm fine with a nursing home—it's payback for all those years I avoided visiting Mom and Pop in the one they lived in." What he thought, but didn't say, was that he could welcome visitors she'd never know about. At home he would have been isolated from his gay community, and, even when Duane visited, they would have carefully chosen their words and topics. In his last six months, he wanted the freedom to be held by the significant men in his life, to tell jokes with friends, and to talk openly about Walther. He wanted, and got, a private room with a solid soundproof door.

Chapter 31

Last Days

Blue-gray walls cast the pallor of death on Dad's pale skin. The nursing home halls echoed loudly as I approached the room, peered around the doorjamb to see if he was breathing, and crossed over to his bed by the window. His whole body rose, then fell, with each labored intake and exhale. I pulled up the heavy naugahyde-covered lounger and sat down as close as I could get. Sensing my presence, he opened his right hand for mine to rest in, or so I believed. He might not have known that it was me. His palm was surprisingly warm and soft. It was uncommon for us to touch, but I left my hand in his. His frail frame was weighed down by sedatives. Sorrow weighed me down. I wondered if he would look like this in death, which would come just two weeks later.

It was mid-May, Mother's Day weekend, and I had flown in from the West Coast to see him and surprise Mother. Marsha came to the airport to meet me and gave me a few minutes alone with him. When she entered the room, we spoke in hushed tones as if we were already in mourning—which we were. He roused a little. She had been trained to get patients up and moving. "Come on, Dad, wake up; look who's here, look whose hand you're holding." His eyelids hesitated, blinked, and then their ocean blue color shone pure and clear. His gaze locked onto my face.

"Hi, Dad." I leaned in and kissed his forehead.

Marsha kept us on task. "Well, did you wonder why they have you dressed today?" He looked down at his navy blue terrycloth robe layered over his signature gray-blue woolen cardigan.

"We're going home for a meal," I said, knowing it would be our last. He pulled his hand away to push himself up.

"Wait, let's raise the bed; that's why you're paying big bucks for this hotel," Marsha said. He winced with pain as he stood upright. Like a wind-up toy, he got moving along rather well.

We headed to the nursing home front desk.

He had become more lighthearted since he'd moved there. When Duane and Doug came to visit, they brought him *Playboy* magazines with the pictures cut out. Mac told them about his secret stash of eight-millimeter gay porn films. To be sure that they wouldn't be found by Alice or "the girls," he told his friends, "I've kept it hidden in a box that says 'old 78's' under the basement stairwell. Sneak them out of the house as soon as you can." He gave Duane his house key and Alice's schedule so that she would most likely be out of the house. But, before they left, they reminisced about Walther, whom my father hoped to see again. "If there is any place like heaven," he said, "we'll meet there."

As Marsha and I escorted Dad to the front office, the nurse on duty looked up from her paperwork and peered at us like we were naughty children. She made us swear that we'd be careful and have him back in time for lights out. As if time mattered. "Don't stay away long, Mac," she told him as she helped us situate him in the car.

"Might not come back, you never know," he told her.

I think that going home for the last time flooded him with trepidation and grief, but he put on a good face. What more could he do as he approached the finish line? He had a daunting list of "if onlys." He had given up on a miracle cure, but he said he wanted to roll the clock back and start his life again. The culture was changing, and if he could start over as a young man in his last decade, I think he would have come fully out of the closet.

We pulled into the curving driveway and parked where he could see the gardens he had long tended. He seemed grateful to have lived long enough to see his yellow tulips emerge from the frosty soil. For years this garden had greeted him when he came home from work. He had spoken to his flowers nearly every evening as he walked the perimeter of the yard to observe every detail. What new shoots were starting, which buds were about to burst? On Saturdays, he used to sit on the grass and pull weeds, with one eye watching the tulips unfold themselves in the warm sunshine. Now he sat in the car and scanned the yard as if he were walking around it and talking to the flowers once again. He had painted a couple of dozen fine water-color pictures, but none of them was as personally satisfying as his garden. We gave him plenty of time to look at it.

"Okay," he said, "let's see what happens when I try to walk across the patio and up the steps." Marsha, with her nursing experience, felt far more confident than I did that he could do this. We set out across the patio with one of us on either side. He seemed steady enough, straightening his back slightly. When we came to the narrow concrete steps, I dropped back and left him in her care. She firmly took his left elbow. On the third step, his right foot refused to cooperate, and the toe of his shoe caught on the rocks that edged the garden. He slid out of her arm too quickly for her to catch him. Down he went. His feet splayed out, he spun halfway around. He knew not to block his fall with fragile wrist bones and rocked backward onto a slope of garden soil. His knees buckled, and his derriere hit the dirt. Sweet woodruff and ivy cushioned him beneath the hawthorn tree he had often cursed for its large thorns.

We were silent, fearing the worst—fearing that the bones in his back and hips, honeycombed from the bone cancer, had just disintegrated under him. He closed his eyes easily and restfully. Was he in pain? We couldn't tell. And then we watched his belly, like the roll of an ocean wave, start to jiggle. His chest expanded, and his chin began to bob as he spasmed with laughter. He rose up on his elbows, still laughing. Tears ran down his cheeks. And he kept laughing. Soon I caught his laugh, then Marsha too. All three of us laughed and cried, sitting together under the hawthorn tree.

Gaining composure, Dad said, "I can think of nothing better than to fall down and die in my own garden! After all these years of digging around in this soil, I might as well become compost." And he laughed again, turning slightly on his side and pushing himself upright. He brushed the dirt off his pants and stretched out each leg to be sure it was working properly.

"Nothing broken?" Marsha asked.

"It doesn't appear to be. Now that's a miracle."

Our laughter must have alerted Mother to our arrival, since she rushed out the back door and over to him.

"What are you doing in the garden, honey? Are you all right?"

And then she unexpectedly saw me. I was "supposed" to be out in California. She turned and wrapped her arms around me, and we all started crying again. Tears of thanks that Dad wasn't all broken apart in the garden, that we could be together, and that we loved each other so very much.

Dad said his goodbye to the rock garden he had fallen into and made peace with the hawthorn tree. We hoisted him to his feet. On Marsha's arm, he made it up the rest of the walkway steps. We plopped him down in his tan chair in the living room and put a blanket on his lap. The *Columbus Citizen Journal* was on a TV tray to the left of him, like old times, but he soon nodded off while we went to the kitchen and prepared the meal.

We ate midday in the formal dining room, and I offered the family prayer that had been Grandpa Chet's: "Lord, for what we are about to receive, make us truly thankful." I tried not to laugh. A few months prior to my visit, a parishioner told me he and his wife pray this prayer before sex. We unfolded our hands and ate the ham mother had defrosted along with microwaved potatoes and frozen green vegetables. It wasn't the holiday feasts of yesteryear; all of the grandparents were gone, too. Grandma Bata, the last of the four of them to go, had passed away quickly in April two years earlier. At her funeral it snowed, and they couldn't bury her for weeks until the ground defrosted. In that mysterious way we think of saints surrounding us, they were all at the table with us. Dad barely touched his small portions. Mother ate well, despite chemotherapy, by taking pills for nausea.

On the wall behind Father's head was a dark oil portrait he had completed in art school. The old fellow had a cane, and his hand resting on top of it was so pale that the painting was hauntingly ghostlike. As a child, I avoided the painting altogether by taking an alternate route to the kitchen from the hallway. The man's sunken eyes stared straight forward. He was gaunt and somber, like an old school master at an orphanage. Act out in the dining room and you'd be sent to live with the old guy, right? Not me, I'll be good. I looked across the table at my thinned and frail father. All the fat on his face was gone, too. But he was not the guy in the oil painting. My father's eyes were kind, not hollow or distant. My father's old face had love in it. I wasn't scared of him. I was drawn to him. I wanted to hold his face in my hands and stare into his eyes like a newborn in the safety of her father's arms. I didn't want his face to go away.

My sister and I carried the bulk of the conversation during our meal, chatting about our jobs and children. Dad would occasionally ask a mundane question and then go back to pushing the food around on his plate. We could sense how tired he was and Mother's growing grief at seeing him like this. She visited him often, but while he was in the hospital, she wandered around the house aimlessly— with no one to cook for or clean up after. No more manhattans over which to review their days. Sometimes she felt fine about her own cancer, because she wouldn't have to live alone for long. Their forty-four years together were coming to a close.

"It's time for me to go back," he said, "or Nurse Ratched will have my head."

Mother raised herself up from her chair and leaned over and kissed his lips.

"Okay, dear, we understand."

I stayed with Mother two more days, visiting Dad every morning when he was alert. Those days unburdened her of many secrets. We perused five huge picture books that spanned their marriage. They previously had hidden meanings written in disappearing ink. Now all could be revealed. Now we could chat about friends she had to keep secrets from and those she trusted and told. She used the term "likely" to describe Dad's close relationships with war buddies, and again described their unsatisfactory sexual experiences. She sipped her coffee and smoked a few puffs, but put the cigarette out. She read sections of Dad's journal from his work with war veterans—the one that she destroyed thereafter. Taking in this whole new world of my parents was like drinking castor oil. I hoped it would cure me, but swallowing and feeling it go down was miserable.

By this time we all knew that Dad was gay. That's the term he used, in the year before his death while talking to my sister's second soon-to-be ex-husband. Her ex reported it to her, commenting, "No wonder you are so screwed up, honey—your dad is gay" or something equally moronic. She confronted Dad, and he confessed with a simple head nod. But I left him safely in secrecy while he was dying. For nearly ten years I'd hinted that he was gay, and he'd evaded my comments for nearly ten years. I was done tango dancing.

On my last day with him, he said, "Honey, this could be genetic, and God forbid you ever get it." I waved this off. My death was a long way off, and I didn't want to think about it. After a long pause he added, "I hope you will forgive me." Forgive you for what? For passing down a slow bone-destroying cancer? Or did he mean forgive him for being in the closet and keeping us all wrapped up in secrets and shame?

Every kid has a list of things to forgive. Dad, I forgive you for having multiple myeloma. I forgive you for always making me wear shoes outside, for your picayune habit of straightening wall pictures when visiting my house, for neglecting church once I grew old enough to go in your place. I forgive you for keeping every letter I wrote home and giving them back to me with spelling corrections on them. It didn't work, by the way; I still can't spell.

I forgive you for the stuff that's harder to forgive, like your detachment from Mom, which left me to be her companion. I just wanted to go on being a kid. You handed the phone to Mother every time I called, and that's forgiven, as well as the year you went home at Christmastime rather than staying with us on the West Coast. You lied to me about freezing pipes, when you were really going back to spend the week with Walther, and I forgive you for that, too. Dad, I know how much you loved him.

I forgive you for hiding, even though I have ached to know all of you. I wanted to ask. You wanted to talk about it. We couldn't get there even at the end. I knew the straight dad, the *Leave It to Beaver* dad, the *Ozzie and Harriet* dad. I wish I had known the gay dad, too. So Dad, whatever you meant when you asked for forgiveness, I offer even more. I've stopped whining. I forgive you.

Chapter 32

The Shiny Blue Casket

Mom's eyebrows were thinned by chemotherapy, and what few hairs remained were pale gray, so her rusty red wig was obviously a throwback to days long ago. She and her hairdresser were conspiring to help her feel young again. As Marsha, Mom, and I walked through the double doors from the casket display room to the main office of Steigner's Funeral Home, her wig slipped slightly to the left. I resisted the temptation to push it back in place.

A tall man in his fifties wearing a dark blue suit annoyingly acted as if he knew us. Waving us into the room, he pulled back a mauve-colored satin chair for my mother to sit down on, and Marsha and I found our own seating. He took his place behind a mahogany desk and pulled out a laminated half sheet listing casket prices. He shuffled it between us like his hand was on a Ouija board, waiting to see which of us would reach for it first. I passed it to Mom, who was too wrapped up in her tears and too tired to reach forward on her own.

"The caskets are very beautiful, Mr. Dunlap," I said, "but my father wanted to be buried in an *old pine box*." I added a slight country twang at that part of the story, "like the ones they used to make by hand."

"He didn't want anyone lining his vault either, as if the worms won't get to him eventually," Marsha added.

Mother perked up a bit and chimed in, "And he didn't want anyone to spend his hard earned money on his funeral."

I slipped my sister the price list. Five thousand to fifteen thousand dollars, depending on adornments, embellishments, and "hood ornaments," we joked afterward.

"Do you have anything more basic?" she asked. Mr. Dunlap, looking pissed off, albeit politely, escorted us in silence to another room, while he extolled the beauty of the unadorned cherry and oak wooden caskets.

"These are beautifully designed," he said, "and they are only twenty-five hundred dollars."

Mother was slowly making her way toward a gray felt casket in the back of the room. Mr. Dunlop flew into action, as if to catch her before she looked any closer.

"Why, my dears, this is just little more than a cardboard box," he stammered. We stood on either side of Mom and hugged her, which started her tears flowing again.

Dunlop was still pitching, "You have to remember, you'll have visitors who come for the viewing and the service itself. You want the casket at the service, too, as I recall. This is the casket we use for the indigent poor."

And that did it. Mom straightened up, dried her eyes with the back of her hand, corrected the tilt of her red wig, and said, "Perfect. We'll take it."

The following Friday we went back to Steigner's Funeral Home to meet family and friends at Dad's viewing. The smell of lilies, roses, and embalming fluid was nauseatingly sweet. I instinctively reached into my pocket for Dad's handkerchief to be ready for sneezing. It was the one that he had given me at my wedding when I began to falter on my vows and he noticed my tears. There were two dead people laid out for viewing on this day, and the suited usher directed us to the left. There, peering past huge bouquets, we saw Mac laid out in a glorious metallic, midnight blue, silver chrome-trimmed casket. Mother grabbed for my elbow, Marsha stood stock-still.

"What do we do about this?" Mother whispered. I offered to go find Mr. Dunlop for a little chat.

On my walk down the hall to the office, I wondered if one of Dad's friends had purchased an upgrade for him as a way to send him out in a style befitting Liberace. Mr. Dunlop seemed sincerely baffled. He had to see this for himself, he said. The viewing room was full of visitors looking at my father's extravagant resting place and consoling Mom as Mr. Dunlop entered the viewing room. I trailed one step behind him.

He stroked his chin and said, "Oh my."

Once the visitors cleared away and we had space to talk, he approached Mother. "Well, there's obviously a mix-up here. We'll fix this for tomorrow's service."

He gestured for me to come with him, and Marsha followed. "I'm so sorry," he said, "but you could pay an upgrade fee, and we could just keep him in this casket."

"Are you kidding?" Marsha asked. He was obviously unaware of our McClintock stubborn streak. Marsha and I pulled up the mauve chairs and put our bodies in them for the sit-in.

"Are you planning to switch Dad into the plain felt casket for the funeral tomorrow after everyone has seen him looking as classy as Liberace tonight?" I asked.

"Well, it would be awkward," he said.

And Marsha, bless her, said right back, "Mr. Dunlop, your staff put him in that shiny blue casket, so you can bury him in it, too . . . at no extra charge."

"We've held every family funeral here for decades," I reminded him.

And Mr. Dunlop agreed to bury his funeral home's best casket with Mac in it at the pauper's price. Dad got his low-cost funeral and cushioned luxury in which to await decay. My unpretentious father, after years of hiding in a modest conventional life, made a fabuloso entry to the Castro District of Heaven. Rumor has it that sometimes when the tulips bloom in spring and all of the paintings in the house are hanging straight as he required them to be, you can hear him singing, "When the roll is called up yonder I'll be there." When I scrunch up my face and close my eyes tightly, I conjure up a picture of him looking ever so much like Fred Astaire in tails and a bow tie. He's in the gay men's chorus along with Tim Mullins who gave him his first lessons in sex, his army buddies, a couple of patients he treated who never overcame their war trauma, Doug Gold from the university, my friend the priest, and next to him of course, his true love Walther P. Michael. They are singing their hearts out, and they are free.

> When the trumpet of the Lord shall sound, and time shall be no more,
> And the morning breaks, eternal, bright and fair;
> When the saved of earth shall gather over on the other shore,
> And the roll is called up yonder, I'll be there.
>
> *Refrain:*
> When the roll is called up yonder,
> When the roll is called up yonder,
> When the roll is called up yonder,
> When the roll is called up yonder, I'll be there.
>
>
> Let us labor for the Master from the dawn till setting sun,
> Let us talk of all His wondrous love and care;
> Then when all of life is over, and our work on earth is done,
> And the roll is called up yonder, I'll be there.
>
> *Refrain:*
> When the roll is called up yonder,
> When the roll is called up yonder,
> When the roll is called up yonder,
> When the roll is called up yonder, I'll be there.

Chapter 33

Saying Goodbye

Steigner's Funeral Chapel was dimly lit. A maudlin recording of "The Old Rugged Cross" and other old hymns played in the background as we entered and sat in the front row. We had not selected the medley. The textured walls emanated beige and pink, chosen to make a dead body look healthy in a casket. I'd seen two grandmothers and one grandfather bathed in this light in the previous ten years. Both grandmothers looked restful and lovely in rosy hues, Grandfather not so much, and Dad had asked that we keep the casket closed so that no one could "gawk" at him during the service. He rested out of the spotlights in his shiny blue box. We avoided the family seating area off to the side behind a curtain. We didn't hide our grief. We were not shoulder-shaking, sobbing mourners. We would not get out of control. We cried steady streams of silent tears.

I doubt that the preacher said exactly the same thing at all the services, but my memory blurs them together: "Neither life nor death, heights nor depths" keeping us from the love of God. The good reverend's words blended into the background. He neither reached great heights nor plumbed philosophical depths for the meaning of life and death. He wasn't a pearly gates preacher, and the Bible never mentions them anyway. Presbyterians make vague references to eternity and are pretty generous about who gets in. Our services are efficiently short.

Afterward Mom, Marsha, and I processed down the center aisle past friends. Mom reached for a few sympathetic hands. We slipped into the black hearse and rode with Dad in the Cadillac-blue casket to the cemetery only ten minutes away. Stepping over gravestones, we walked solemnly to white folding chairs, set out on runners of plastic grass, Mom first, then Marsha, then me. Dad's casket came forward in the capable hands of Duane and his partner, our back-door neighbor, and Dad's insurance agent/friend Bob Murray, with the funeral director at the back. They settled the casket on a metal support structure over the hole. The hood of Dad's luxurious casket looked like a pool of water as I looked across it. I was drawn back to a place called the Blue Hole near Lake Erie that we visited when I was eight years old, a vertical cave that my parents told me was the deepest hole anywhere in the world, so deep they couldn't even measure it. My vision blurred over the same azure blue, but I could see the dirt at the bottom of the grave, unmistakably final.

Once everyone had found their seats, the funeral staff stepped back and the minister stepped forward. It was June and muggy, and though he had on a tie, his dress shirt was short sleeved. Rev. Bruce had a little black book of rituals in his hand.

He read, "Ashes to ashes, dust to dust."

I was sitting on top of Grandma Bata's gravestone, wondering what her body, now ten years under the topsoil, might look like. I was sitting in full view of the headstones for my grandparents on both sides: Bata, then Sam, who was the first to die of cancer, and then Chet and Clara. All of them side by side, as close in death as they had been in life—all because Charles had made a life-long commitment to Alice and expanded our family. We were like the tall redwood trees that survive because their roots entwine beneath the earth. Standing over their graves one year on Memorial Day, Dad said they should have been laid out with their feet touching—a foursome for bridge so they could play their weekly game in heaven. And when he got sick he said, "Well now I can sub in at the bridge table." We thought of heaven as that kind of place, where you could all be, together again, go on doing what you loved, and be even happier doing it.

My sister and I were assigned the task of going to the cemetery to pick out plots for our parents soon after Dad was diagnosed with multiple myeloma. Mother was too sad and numb to go along. Our first stop that day was the four graves in a row, Mother's parents and Dad's parents all laid out together. A single granite headstone displays their names in Old English lettering. No epitaphs, no carved angels, no vase holder for plastic or decaying flowers. It's very lovely, nonetheless. We stood in the cool fall breeze and spoke silently to them. Maybe my sister told them to keep an eye out for Dad, who was on his way, too soon from our viewpoint. I simply said thanks, keep watching over us, and I miss you.

Finishing communion with the grandparents, we went to the office to buy two more plots. The place was set up like a department of motor vehicles office, with one long counter. As the door closed behind us, a bell rang and a dwarfish man in his sixties with dark-rimmed glasses and weathered hands emerged. His smile warmed his otherwise haggard face.

"What can I do for you ladies today?"

"Well . . . we're here to purchase grave plots for our parents."

"Okay." He got out several large scrapbooks with plastic covers over pages of plots. "Anyone you know already here?"

You'd think we were at the Bellagio Hotel front desk attending a bachelorette party. My sister chimed in, "Actually, all four of our grandparents are buried in a section near the apartment buildings. Any chance we could lay Dad and Mom to rest there, too?"

"Oh, I don't think so. That's the old section. Most of those plots were purchased years ago." He looked over his bifocals at our deflation. "Well, let's have a look anyway," he said. He hoisted out the correct book, and we could see plots defined by bold black lines. Purchased sections were colored in with magic markers. He identified our grandparents' graves and drew a magnifying glass out of a drawer. "Well, well . . . well . . . well. Look here." He pointed to the plots, and we leaned forward. "When these were filled in, the ink ran, and it ran right onto two more plots at the end of the row, right next to your family, so nobody ever bought them. You girls have some kind of luck," he said, "some kind of luck." Dad could sub-in for bridge in the "old section" of the graveyard. We paid whatever he asked and went home to tell Mother the good news.

Sitting next to her now, I could only guess her thoughts. She had advanced stage four oat-cell carcinoma in both lungs. Death was drawing nearer every breath as she sat in full view of her own resting place. The minister continued the service. He closed his worship book, because he knew the last prayer by heart.

"And now with the confidence of children of God . . . let us pray." I mouthed the words while I pleaded with God to heal my mother.

When I looked up, the minister had moved over to the left of the tent, and the funeral home director stood in his place, flushed and damp in his black suit. He gave Mom the already folded American flag. She tucked it under her arm and, consummate hostess that she was, got up and turned to greet guests. I was heading toward the minister's side of the tent to thank and pay him, but Dad's tract-distributing brother Donald blocked my way.

"Do you really think my brother has escaped hell?" he asked the minister. "I know he smoked and played cards. I'd hoped to see him in eternity, but I'm not sure he's made it there." My head was pounding.

"And what if he was also *gay*?" I wanted so badly to shout at him.

I stayed silent; we always stayed silent. Rev. Bruce said calmly, "Mac was one of the most faithful Christian men I have ever known. I have no doubt that he's already been welcomed home to be with Jesus."

What had Dad told, or not told, Rev. Bruce? He reached forward and patted my sullen uncle on the back, then walked around him, shaking his head, and reached for me with open arms.

Chapter 34

The Wake

Our last family home was the split-level house that sat at a low spot on the street, which during our high school years gave my sister and me great views all the way down to both ends of the block but became troublesome in torrential rains. As the street filled with water, it rushed down into our driveway, entered the den, and like a nosy neighbor, let itself right on into the basement. My father had his ego invested in the undulating front lawn. He took so much pride in his cross-hatched patterns across the pure green grass that we were forbidden to run around on it and never (since my sister and I were *girls*) permitted to cut it. The only person he'd let cut it during his illness was Duane, who said, "I could never get it right—not the way he wanted it; I think I crossed over my own paths too many times."

The house sat back off the street by a good twenty yards, and the front sidewalk curved gently up to the house from the driveway. A street lamp stood as a sentinel near two steps at the end of the walkway. On this day, the day of my father's funeral, the sun was bright and fading the remains of daffodils and tulips he had cheerfully planted round the lamppost. I'd escaped from the house and gone to this spot with my plate of tiny pimento-cheese sandwiches, crinkled chips, and gherkins, while mourners inside consoled my mother, tilted their heads, and sighed sympathetically.

A few minutes later, my father's tall and lanky friend Duane sat himself down next to me without asking, or speaking any words at all. He had apparently skipped the food table and come out empty handed. In a crowd of my parents' friends who were social golfers, insurance salesmen, investment analysts, and bridge players—all of them politically conservative and very straight, conversation was safer for us on the front lawn.

This was the first time I had ever been alone with Duane. We both held the silence for a long while, me munching and Duane just leaning back on his long arms as if the beach and ocean waves were stretched out before us instead of the gray asphalt of a suburban street. "Would you please say out loud that my father was gay?" I asked. No introduction, no banter, no subtleties left in me . . . I was also wracked with grief.

"Your father was gay," he said, looking at me kindly without flinching. I returned my eyes to the sidewalk cracks below my feet. I waited while the tears that blurred my vision were absorbed again by my weary eyes.

"Did he die of AIDS?"

He paused a moment and said, "No, I don't think so."

What did he mean by "think"? I needed him to be sure. I had spent much of my life putting together fragments of my father's past. The oncologist in charge of my father's two-year illness couldn't be trusted. Like many other doctors, he might have lied on the death certificate to save my father's honor.

In the mid-1980s, denial among gay men and their families was as epidemic as AIDS itself. Cover-ups were the norm. Many death certificates were recorded as "cancer" or "tuberculosis" to protect the family from the stigma of a loved one's dying of the "gay plague." Parents said their sons were dying of something else, anything else that was fatal, guarding their secrecy. The story was repeated so convincingly that many of them *believed* it was only cancer, while watching the skin lesions of Kaposi's sarcoma take over the bodies of their sweet boys, ignoring the dementia as if it didn't mean that it was truly AIDS. Some families totally ignored a gay partner's care-giving, and hospitals refused visitation rights for lifelong companions. I understood their denial.

Why couldn't I go ahead and believe my father's stated diagnosis? Dad had even apologized to me for his bone marrow cancer. "This could be genetic, honey," he had said, pausing when he was very frail and short of breath.

Okay, so maybe it wasn't AIDS. Maybe I wanted it to be. Maybe that would have confirmed everything and made it clear that he was more than friends with Walther. My sister and I could have gotten truly pissed off at him for getting it, for taking risks like that. It would have been evidence that he had gay sex partners. Here at the funeral post-game show, I was determined to ask questions I'd wanted to ask for a long time. I wanted to say things I wouldn't have said with him around. Since I had spent at least thirty years *not* thinking Dad was gay, I just needed someone else to say the words we hadn't been allowed to say.

Duane sensed the desperation in my questions and was patient and quiet for a long while. "He would have told me," he said. "I would have known." Maybe everyone around Dad had doubts about the truth of things. I thought Duane knew everything. He knew the underground world of gay men that my father inhabited.

What else did Duane know? Names of lovers, places of trysts, and the man named Walther. And then, without warning, I lost my courage. I didn't ask him anything more. I'd become so shamed for asking and so accustomed to not knowing that I shut down automatically like an old camera with a very slow shutter speed. Duane and I sat in silence for a long while, as the warmth of the early summer sun filled in the space left by the silence.

For thirty years we had all tolerated my father's private world. In our family, curiosity was dangerous. We called it respect—our not asking was respect. We called it his right to privacy. We called it loyalty. And here on the steps, as he journeyed to wherever dead fathers go, two questions were all I asked. They took everything out of me, like a ride at the fun center where you spin and spin and eventually the floor drops out and leaves you pressed flat to the side walls. You came away happy if you didn't barf while you were in it. Talking to

Duane defied all of the forces of the family energy field. So I left it there.

I turned to Duane after another prolonged silence. "Thank you for being his friend," I said. I knew him to have been a caring and supportive influence—a friend who made Dad feel safe enough to crack open the door of his closet and breathe after a very long life of stifling confinement. Duane wrapped his arms around me, and I leaned into him. For the rest of my life I would miss the feel of a six-foot tall man with generous arms. I got up and mumbled something about an obligation to go back inside to visit with Mom and other family members, who were eating post-funeral crustless sandwiches. Ever the dutiful daughter, I left Duane sitting on the steps in my father's perfectly groomed front yard.

Chapter 35

Mom Comes Out at Last

"I guess it's time you knew the truth," she said. We were sitting on vinyl-cushioned lawn furniture on the back porch the evening after the funeral. The June air was moist, and the screens were dotted with bugs. Across the back lawn, fireflies winked on and off in Dad's favorite garden beds. "Your father was gay. There, I said it." She took in a gulp of air. "'Been wanting to tell you for years, but I just couldn't do it. Some things just have to wait." I said nothing.

"I think it was his mother, really," she continued. "She wanted a girl, and he knew it. He overheard her say it, if I remember it right. So she dressed him up in little frilly outfits. He wore pantaloons and pinafores, things like that. That's probably where it started." Her face was gaunt from chemotherapy as her lung cancer relentlessly threatened every breath. I wanted to refute her misguided theories that Grandma could have made him gay by cross-dressing him or by her regrets, but research seemed out of place at that moment. She lit another cigarette.

I was relieved that the breeze blew the smoke off the porch behind her.

"Marsha learned about it when she and Judd were breaking up. Your father told Judd about it. My heavens, I hope he didn't have anything going with Judd."

The thought of my father losing all grip on morality confounded me.

"Mom, I can't believe he'd do that."

"Honey, there's a lot you wouldn't believe."

"Try me, Mom."

"Like our trip to Europe, remember that? Remember when I told you about the woman with the tassels? Well, there's more to the story than that. It wasn't the trip of our dreams," she said. "Do you want to know what it was really like?" I was thirty-four years old, with my father in the grave and mother sick with lung cancer. She had decided that it was time to say more.

"Sure," I said.

"Daytimes were okay. We'd go to see things, though I got tired of so many museums. We'd have long days on our feet, and then your father went out every evening." She called him "your father," as if they had been legally divorced, rather than just emotionally so. "He'd given up lying to me. He told me he was hoping to find the underground world of gay bars and nightclubs." She lit up and inhaled slowly. "'Maybe I'll get lucky,' he'd said, which meant he'd have sex with someone if he could. I knew he'd come home by early morning, but I didn't get much sleep. I watched the clock for hours, wondering if he was in trouble somewhere, catching a deadly disease, or lying in an alley someplace. By the time he got back to the hotel, I was usually sound asleep. We didn't talk about what he'd been up to."

"Mom, you put up with all this?"

"I wasn't going to leave him. That's just not me. Once it was clear that he only wanted to be with men, I settled for what I could get."

"When did you figure this out?"

"People can choose not to see what's right in front of them. We were young, and we were in love at the beginning. We wanted what everyone wanted back then—a little house in a nice area near good schools where we could raise a family. Our parents became such good friends that our marriage just seemed inevitable—like part of God's plan for us."

"Grandma Bata has always been smitten with Dad."

"I wanted to make her happy and marry someone she respected. Mac had all that. He was easy to talk to, like my girlfriends. He was gentler than other men. I never liked the manly ones who puffed themselves up around girls. They intimidated me. Your father was bright, but he wasn't a know-it-all. He had stunning blue eyes and the silkiest softest hair I'd ever touched. There's a lot you overlook when you have stars in your eyes." She let herself cry a while.

I noticed the North Star with the Big Dipper trailing behind it. "You were good together," I said as I searched for some way to console her. "I asked this before, but when did you really know about him?" Awkwardly talking about Dad's secrets, I avoided the words *gay* or *homosexual*.

"Well, honey," she slowly inhaled fresher air, "I guess part of me knew it all along—but I couldn't deny it when he fell in love with Walther."

"The blue painting was Walther's, wasn't it?" When I asked this, she struggled to inhale and then nodded. No wonder she gave it to Duane on the day after Dad died.

"I never liked that painting. It was dark and odd. I'm sorry, sweetie. It was probably worth a lot of money, and I guess you could have inherited it, but I wanted it gone. And I know Mac wanted Duane to have it."

"Why didn't you give it back to Walther?"

"Oh, my dear, I guess there are a lot of gaps in this story. Walther was dead by then." She switched her legs from left over right to right over left. "Are you comfortable in that chair? Do you want to hear more?"

"Yes, and I think so."

"Your father and Walther went to New York together every year, not just for the theater and museums."

"And they were lovers," I said, since she wouldn't have.

She winced as if I had slapped her across the face. I continued to circumvent her pain. "I know, because I was jealous. Dad had promised to visit New York with me some year, but he didn't live long enough for us to do that."

This time I was the one crying. "I'm going to get a box of tissues." I came back out with a couple of glasses of water, too, and Mom picked up where she'd left off.

"Walther died in a small plane crash over South America. I hate to say this, but I was relieved. I know Mac loved him, but keeping their secret exhausted me. When he died, I thought I'd have some of your father back, but it didn't turn out that way. He sat in his chair in your sister's old bedroom and thumbed through every page of the Time Life art books on Matisse and Renoir and Van Gogh. I think he stared at the pages until he crawled into them. He was off at the countryside at Arles, or sitting by a pond of water lilies. Since he loved his garden, he was probably sitting in that Van Gogh painting with the little girl and the watering can. I don't know where he went, really. He lived up in that room with the door closed. I could sometimes hear him crying. He was living in this house, but he was gone. He slept in there, too, except when you visited home. Then we made it look like we were still sleeping together in the big bedroom."

"Oh, Mom, I'm so sorry."

"Remember when he gained all that weight after he stopped smoking and then lost it all again? He got so thin because he stopped eating after Walther died. I'd coax him to eat and then watch him pick around at his food and push back from the table, with his usual 'thank you, honey.' Watching him grieve was so painful, and all I could offer him was comfort food and distractingly cheerful chatter. At his request I stopped making manhattans. He'd go upstairs to sit with that ridiculous painting with the bare-breasted woman who looked like a hooker. And I could never understand what he saw in it. I wanted it out of this house, and it sure felt good to give it away."

I listened numbly, retreating to the back of my own head. I felt nothing but guilt. I'd helped hundreds of people in their isolated grief over lovers, friends, and family members who died in the AIDS epidemic, and I wasn't even aware of my own father's months in mourning. While I was on the West Coast raising my daughter, surviving my husband's betrayals, and piecing our marriage back together over and over again, my parents were no longer dancing in the living room—they were giving each other wide berths to avoid further bruising.

And there sat my mother on the day after we buried him, telling me that I had never really known the man I call my father. I knew the straight man, but I didn't know the gay man. I knew the loyal man, but I didn't know the adulterer. I knew the level-headed, practical man, but I had only glimpsed the artist at his easel, the interior designer with his color swatches, the theatrical mustached villain. I didn't know the unabashed, passionate lover, the man whose friends might have called him a *dally omi-palone* (a sweet homosexual), using gay speak in the early 1960s. Apparently, he was all of these as well. Just one day past his funeral, my mother, who had lost him so many times she stopped counting, faced her final loss and unburdened herself to me. That was the day she came all the way out of my father's closet.

Chapter 36

The Bust

When Marsha came down the stairs looking for me, I was hidden behind a pile of boxes in the basement.

"Are these vintage yet?" she asked, her bent arm covered with fluttering wide ties.

"Why didn't she toss those out?" I asked.

"Why did they keep any of this?" Marsha flung Dad's balled up socks into a box.

I had taken a week off from work and flown back to Ohio to help her pack and clear the house. Mom sat upstairs on the green couch, not smoking, painfully breathing shallow breaths and sipping tepid Folgers coffee. Watching us dismantle everything she'd found familiar for twenty-five years, her gaze was distant and frozen, I guess she was using her well-honed dissociation skills.

We climbed the stairs to check on her.

"How ya doin,' Mom?"

I stretched out on the tan carpet to ease the ache in my back. Marsha collapsed onto the couch next to Mom, scanning the room for things to pack. My oil painting of Dad's backyard daisies had been taken down, leaving its faded shadow and a nail. Dad's Blenko glass collection was boxed in bubble wrap. The bookshelves were bare. Mom pointed to the only artwork left in the room, her hand shaking slightly.

"Well," she said, "what do you suggest we do with that?"

"That" was a life-size plaster bust of a man we didn't know, mounted on a four-foot-tall, Dad-designed pedestal. From time to time, the family made up stories about him: Cicero about to make a speech, Einstein prominently displayed at the Metropolitan Museum of Art, a hologram in Disney's Haunted House. But in reality, he was a random middle-aged fellow who occasionally modeled in Dad's sculpture class—hair askew, bulging stone cold eyes, a slightly broken nose, and skinny lips. His neck draped down like fabric over a steel rod on which he was mounted. Normally self-critical about his artwork, at parties Dad told his friends that this bust was his finest achievement.

"Nothing to write home about, right?"

Mom's joke revealed her secretly harbored distaste for it all these years. Her smile was bittersweet. Marsha and I had always hated it. For a moment, we were all young again, three chortling girls with impeccable taste.

"I guess we'll have to give it away, or something," I said, laughing so hard I was crying. When the furniture movers came later that day to pick up the things Mom would need in her new assisted living apartment, the couch went, too. Everything was cleared from the living room except the old man's bust.

"Hey, lady," the moving guy said, "this is really cool. Is it going to a museum or something?" Mother shot a quick glance at us and raised one eyebrow. We smiled and nodded.

"Nope," she said, "Do you really like it?"

"Absolutely!"

"Then it's yours."

After he left, Marsha and I walked Mother downstairs with us and plopped her onto a folding chair so she could direct artifacts to one of several boxes labeled *Trash, Goodwill, Marsha,* and *Karen.* Dad's art supplies went into the box with my name on it—a collapsible easel Dad was given at his quickly thrown retirement party but never used, silk screens, frames, canvas rolls, along with papers, notebooks, certificates, and family scrapbooks. I paused and opened a black journal with a fire-red spiral binding and an embossed silver eagle on the cover. On the first page I saw Mom's name in Dad's handwriting—his Christmas card list, 1938. She smiled.

"Dad's journal?" I raised one eyebrow.

"Put that one in your box, sweetie." She grabbed a three-ring binder and threw it in, too.

Before the day was out, Mom put her bulky jewelry case on her lap, opened it, and distributed gold chains, ruby rings, the circle pin Dad had given her on an anniversary, the silver rose he had commissioned for their fortieth. She was letting it all go. And I had to get back home to my congregation and family.

She moved into an apartment that provided meals, company, and comfort. The gift trip she'd given me with my husband to Hawaii wasn't what any of us had hoped for. And when I arrived on the mainland at the San Francisco airport and entered the building, I was greeted by an airline hostess.

"Your friend Kim called to notify you that your mother has gotten worse and you need to fly directly to Ohio." She handed me a one-way ticket to Columbus that my sister had purchased, arranged to have my luggage sent along, and walked me to the next plane. I headed east, and my husband went north to rejoin our daughter Megan.

On the stop-over in Chicago, I called my sister and knew by her tone of voice.

"I'm sorry, Karen—you didn't make it, but she knew you were on your way—that you were coming to hold me up, so that we could get through this together."

Like orphan children, I thought, but didn't say. She died on Thursday in holy week, and I was back in the pulpit on Easter Sunday, preaching Jesus' rising as evidence for eternal life, hoping like heck I'd see my mother again someday.

In a few months, the boxes I shipped to myself arrived on my doorstep at the parsonage I shared with my husband in California. Unopened, we moved them with us to our next parsonage where they sat for ten years, to be moved again after a process server knocked on the front door and handed me divorce papers. I took the papers and steadied myself against the door jam. The divorce hit me like the earthquakes I'd been through in the same town, and required the same survival strategies—leave essentials behind, connect with loved ones at a safe location, and let people know you are all right. I wasn't all right. I was facing the painful truth that I had lived my mother's life—completely willing to cover up secrets, spending years mired in shame.

Once the ground stopped shaking, I did all that anyone can do after an earthquake—I got up and assessed the damage. I ended up with half the stuff that we had accumulated during our marriage and reluctantly became a half-time parent. The church I was called to serve needed more than I could offer, and I needed more than they could provide, so after two years, I packed everything yet again and took the road north to Ashland, Oregon, where I'd purchased a home with my parents' estate. On summer nights under the stars at our regional Shakespeare festival, Megan, about to enter high school, was enthralled.

"Mom," she noted when *King Lear* was over, "the actress didn't sound like she was really grieving." She was already hooked on theater, and too well acquainted with grief.

I moved the old boxes I'd shipped to myself four times in eighteen years without opening them. Too caught up in grief after losing both parents and my marriage in a few short years, I couldn't emotionally afford nostalgia—I had to focus on survival. In the Hmong tradition, an ancient oral story among nomadic farmers goes like this: When someone dies, rotating family members drag the coffin of their loved one with them from community to community as they move every season, finding new land on which to plant and harvest. A thick metal chain is wrapped around the wooden box and looped around the person who drags it. On and on it bounces over rough ground, through rain-soaked potholes, until at last the chain breaks. And when it does, that is where you bury it.

Twelve years went by after my divorce until I met a man without secrets. He had abundant love and very little shame, so I married him. We moved to our new house in 2005. Soon thereafter, a lighting contractor we had hired called me out to the garage for a brief inspection. "I'm sorry, lady," he said, "but your garage ceiling is sagging so badly I can't install the new fixtures. You may want to move stuff out of the attic before it gets worse and falls in on you," he har-rumphed, and walked off the job.

The previous month when I was traveling, my husband told me he "cleaned out the garage," which I thought meant "threw out old stuff." But it turned out that he just hoisted boxes, bins, and lawn furniture up the rickety wooden drop-down stairs and stacked it all on the ceiling beams. At the time, I was fuming, and our exchange about the situation was comical. Picture a cartoon of Minnie and Mickey rolling around in the dust with stars and exclamation points exploding over their heads and then walking away arm and arm like old friends. The problem soon became an unexpected blessing.

The very next Saturday, we hauled everything down and I faced a garage full of memories, among them the box that still had my parents' old Columbus, Ohio, address on the label. I let it tilt against my belly, pulled back the flaps, and reached in to find a small box full of faded letters my parents sent to each other in the first years of their young love. Marsha had already spent years reading through boxes of letters she'd taken after the funeral. What secrets did *these* letters hold? Why had Mother kept them? The letters contained runes that I needed an advanced degree to interpret. The rest of the box was filled with Dad's art supplies: silk screens, ink, paints and brushes. I called my sister the next morning.

"Do you remember anything about old journals Dad kept?"

"Only one," she said, "from the war years when he worked at a military hospital helping guys with trauma recovery." It came back to me in memory fragments.

"Did you read that journal?"

"No, Mother had it in her lap one day, and she described it as very depressing—I think she threw it out. I also vaguely recall seeing another black journal."

I went back to the garage and searched to the very bottom of the box, and there lay the American Sterilizer journal and a standard blue three-ring binder of lined pages. These diaries covered his court-ship with Mom, his lesson from Tim, their marriage, and World War II. With those three years in place, the rest of his life came into focus, and I found not only the loyal married father he had been, but the gay man, belatedly revealed.

Chapter 37

National Coming Out Day

Since it was an Oregon fall evening, the odds are pretty high that my memory is right about driving in a downpour. But memory has so much uncertainty to it, particularly if you learn, as I did, that the truth is like a laser pointer—it causes damage if held too long on one point and is fascinatingly distracting when it moves around a lot. The blue Jetta I was driving to church that night was ten years old and leaked when it rained from the disintegration of the rubber stripping around doors. The carpet in the trunk sprouted hundreds of little green starts from a bag of bird seed that split open the preceding summer, and the wetness inside and out made me feel like a local after years of living in California sunshine.

I was trembling like I do when I get cold, with a slight stomach-ache that forebodes an ulcer in the making, and I had the car heater cranked up as high as it would go. I was about to fulfill a promise I made to God two years earlier that if She wanted me to continue serving her people in my career as pastor of local churches, she'd have to lead me to a church where everyone was welcome, where a quirky family like the one I grew up in could be out of secrecy and still have an honored place in a pew.

For several weeks I planned for this next step. My therapist sent me to a workshop at the Self & Soul Center to learn about super ego defense strategies, and I practiced what I learned. I said, "I am taking time off from work, so back off!" when the tyrant voice in my head would drag me toward codependency (a trait I inherited from my mother). I said this three times with growing adamancy. By the third time, I screamed so loudly it hurt my vocal cords. Sometimes the tyrant pushed me to exhaust myself, and I said, "I didn't visit that parishioner in the hospital today, and it's alright with me!" repeating my defense three times until I was hoarse. The car seemed to be the best place for this exercise, because I could be alone and do this yelling without scaring any of the pets or people back at the house; the car was a safe haven for my emotions, especially in a downpour.

Halfway to the meeting, the terror of jeopardizing my job and the force field of so many years in a closeted family increased, and what started out as my knees trembling became all-out shaking. I hung on more tightly to the steering wheel. My eyes flooded with tears, and I yelled at my long-dead parents, "I'm talking about it, and it's okay with me." I was intent on repeating the defenses like a mantra until the crying stopped, or the rain stopped, or both.

The board of directors meeting fell on the first National Coming Out Day, 1998, and I was about to come out of my father's closet.

Uncomfortable folding chairs lined four eight-foot folding tables in the social hall. A dozen leaders in the congregation arrived on time, greeted each other warmly but wasted little time settling in. After approving minutes and listening to reports from committee members, the chairwoman turned to me for my section of the meeting.

"Today is National Coming Out Day," I said, and all fiddling with pens and foot shuffling stopped instantly. I took in the looks on their faces and wondered if, had it been *my* story I was about to tell, had it been *my* coming out day—all hell would have broken loose. It's these moments without words, when chests tighten and air is sucked out of rooms, that keep people in the closet way too long.

"I just want to say tonight that my father was gay, and he lived with my mother up until both of them died some years back. I feel compelled to start talking about it with you and with other people in the congregation."

To my left, a balding man in his early seventies wearing a tweed sports coat cleared his throat and began, "Well, since it is National Coming Out Day, I'd like to tell those of you who don't already know that my son Danny is gay and he has a partner, Bart, and they are very much in love. . . . Of course it's taken us quite a few years to come to grips with it—I wish they had a church they could go to in their town."

Across the table, a rancher and avid hiker in his late fifties said, "We've got to start letting people know that this is an inclusive church, rather than just a 'friendly' congregation."

I watched an elderly woman to my right start to shrink up and back away from the table. "Nelda," I said, "what are you thinking?"

"I'm thinking that people will stop pledging and that the Bible says that homosexuality is WRONG."

"Would you like to know how I sum that up?" I asked.

"Okay," she said in a whisper.

"I think that back in Leviticus it was all about the preservation of male seed (technically, sperm) and that creating offspring was the ethic; therefore no masturbation, no sex with animals, no 'spilling of seed' anywhere that wouldn't produce babies. So, they made laws about sex to fit their need to create offspring within their faith. It makes sense, doesn't it? But Jesus was all about the ethic of love— plain and simple, along with some other ethics about keeping promises, remaining faithful to one another, suspending judgment, and welcoming the outcast. I think God loved my gay father like crazy and loves me that way, too, and all of you that way, too."

Nelda was silent, but other people were nodding their heads. I knew they'd been recently challenged by a man named Keith who'd been coming to church as a woman named Katie. When she began singing in the choir, a well-heeled tithing member who sat next to her became repulsed and withdrew her membership. Other members were relieved and considered the issue settled.

"We're blessed by her," the chairman said. "There's a place at the table for everyone!" And that is the moment when they offered me a place among them, too, despite my anxieties about truth-telling and my seemingly one-of-a-kind family.

A month after this meeting, the phone rang in the church office, and a woman named Brenda asked me if we perform holy unions at the church. She'd been turned down by other clergy and congregations in our community. I had "married" a clergy friend and her partner nearly twenty years earlier, before the prohibitions were voted into church law. But this time I was particularly motivated to say *yes* when I learned that Brenda and her partner were raising kids. Anyone denying those mothers the right to be married would have been heaping more shame upon the children. I wouldn't shame the kids—I knew the pain of inherited homophobia very personally. After consulting my colleague on staff, we planned to co-officiate the ceremony. We consciously treated the wedding like any other in preparation and protocol.

The Wednesday before the Saturday wedding, the office secretary picked up a call from the local television news station asking if we were going to marry a lesbian couple. An emergency meeting of the board was convened. A few people were irate that they hadn't been told about the ceremony, though I pointed out that they were not informed about the weddings of heterosexuals in the congregation, and that the pastors were given full discretion to marry whomever they chose to marry. The member of the board who had single-handedly been paying a third of the budget for salaries said he was withdrawing his membership immediately. Others, though, were so supportive that they made a plan to set up a room in the building for reporters to come for interviews, with coffee and snacks. They recruited people to walk around the outside of the building and make sure that the wedding itself was not disturbed by intruders and planned to invite any protestors inside for coffee and doughnuts while they talked about their understanding of Jesus' all-encompassing love. They became the hands and feet of Jesus that day and surrounded the sanctuary for the ceremony that would legitimate a family.

A few weeks after the ceremony, so many members left the church or withheld pledges that the board chairwoman said they could no longer pay my salary. The secretary's hours were reduced, and the janitor was laid off. My colleague, the senior member of the staff, updated his teaching license and worked as a substitute in the schools, trying to hold everything together. I was a single mom, with a daughter I'd promised not to uproot during her high school years, so I went on unemployment and looked into career alternatives.

After sleeping restlessly for days, I had a dream on the night before an interview for a job that I didn't want to take. My clergy vestments, robe, and stoles were hanging on a wooden fence. Flood-waters were rising in the creek behind the fence, about to over-take a little wooden shack in which I lived. In the dream, I'd gotten my daughter to safety and run up the hill myself. I awoke looking down into the valley and seeing that fence about to go under water and take away the identity I'd had for twenty years. My heart was pounding, and the impulse was clear to me. I had to go back and retrieve them, even if it meant getting swept away.

The next morning, I called a colleague who ran a counseling cen-ter in our area. He met me for lunch later that same week and heard the story of my dream. Their program could use me, he said, and I could start by answering phones in the office for minimum wage while I went back to school for a counseling degree. Meanwhile I could lead grief groups and take on some clients with private pay who were looking for pastoral counseling. My doctoral program covered the cost of my work through a federal grant, and my next five years I preserved my pastoral identity while achieving a PhD and becoming a licensed psychologist.

The day I stood in my garage and opened the box marked Havi-land Road, Columbus, Ohio, and pulled out Dad's black journal, I also found my birth certificate tucked into a mailing envelope. Carl Jung, Anna Freud, Richard Bowlby, and other historic figures in the history of psychology had led me to study the complexity of the unconscious mind and the ways that children repeat their parents' unfinished or unconscious lives. Even though I'd seen my birth cer-tificate a few times, that day I stopped and actually read it—closely. Under my father's occupation on my birth certificate was the word "psychologist." While I knew he'd studied psychology, he'd never called himself a psychologist. After I'd earned a PhD in psychol-ogy, published a dissertation on the effects of closeted gay and lesbian parents on offspring, written three books on secrets and sexual shame, and spent fifteen years working in the field, I finally owned up to following in my father's footsteps. The credentials and degrees weren't the point; I did it all to liberate us both from shame.

I'd told God some years back that I would spread the word about the thousands of unobservable children who live in families with closeted parents and what it is like for them to live under a cloud of cultural shame. I have had many conversations with colleagues and clients in order to understand the subtle uniqueness shared by children of the closet. And then I confessed to my women's writing group that I had been avoiding the one story I had wanted to tell for the past fifteen years—the hardest story of all—the story of my father's closet. More than simply the relief of telling, by writing the book I got to know, and sometimes fill in the blanks for, my quirky lovable father. Writing the story would mend my heart and keep me close to my parents, whose secrets and cancer took them to their graves far too early. It led me past my yearning for the father I didn't know and finally healed my soul.

Epilogue

On my way to New York for a national conference, I was moody and restless. As an anxious flyer, I expect air travel to stir up my central nervous system, but the skies were clear heading east from Portland, Oregon, over the Rockies. Somewhere above a flat prairie state, the malaise deepened. My father's vague promise to meet me for theater in New York left me yearning for him. My inside-kid just wanted like all get-out to be sitting next to Daddy. I sadly didn't imagine my long-dead father joining me in New York.

Back in my late thirties, when he was newly retired, I still believed our New York rendezvous could happen. I'd fly in from the West Coast and, coming down the jet-way, I'd see him above the crowds, catch his eye, and be reassured by his warm smile. We'd go see a show every night for a week, walk around Times Square until midnight, and then find a place to go dancing. What I didn't know is that my imagined trip was impossible after Walther's death. Dad couldn't have looked at a playbill without feeling Walther next to him. It would have caused him great pain to be back there without Walther, visiting their romantic old haunts. Dad's grief would have "outed" him.

Instead, I met Megan in New York. Theater has become her life. She went to college on a theater scholarship and has climbed the ranks in Bay Area theaters to become a stage manager. Since she has very little time off, it seemed like a minor miracle that she could join me.

I brought tickets with me for *The Book of Mormon.* We also planned to see *You Can't Take It with You,* since Dad once played the grandfather role and the current production starred James Earl Jones, whom I long ago sat next to at the Peace Church. I also ordered tickets for the revival of *Pippin,* and Megan's step-sister, who lives in the Bronx, was holding them for us. Megan met her for dinner and picked up the tickets for our evening show. Walking to meet me outside the theater, she waved the ticket envelope wildly in the air.

"Mom, look," she said, opening the envelope and pulling out the tickets. I stared down at them to read, in bold print, the name *Charles McClintock.*

"How'd that happen?" she asked. I was puzzled and shaken.

"I have no idea. I ordered the tickets online, in my name, with my credit card."

"Wow, Mom, this is so amazing."

"Can we just say it's a bit of Broadway magic?"

"I'm keeping the tickets as evidence," she said, and likely will for her whole life.

My father found a way to make good on his promise by putting his name on our tickets to a play we all loved, and met me in New York after all.

PIPPIN TICKETS